Leadership Skills in Policin

Leadership Skills in Policing

Dr Colin Rogers

OXFORD
UNIVERSITY PRESS

*This book has been printed digitally and produced in a standard specification
in order to ensure its continuing availability*

OXFORD
UNIVERSITY PRESS

Great Clarendon Street, Oxford OX2 6DP
United Kingdom

Oxford University Press is a department of the University of Oxford.
It furthers the University's objective of excellence in research, scholarship,
and education by publishing worldwide. Oxford is a registered trade mark of
Oxford University Press in the UK and in certain other countries

© Colin Rogers 2008

British Library Cataloguing in Publication Data
Data available

Library of Congress Cataloging in Publication Data
Data available

ISBN 978-0-19-953951-2

Cover photos: © ImageSource / Punchstock; iD-8 Photography; Brand X Pictures /
Punchstock; ImageState / Punchstock; UpThe Resolution (uptheres) / Alamy;
Justin Kase / Alamy; Mike Abrahams / Alamy; Chris George / Alamy; David
Lawrence / Alamy; Dominic Harrison / Alamy; Up The Resolution (uptheres) /
Alamy; Photodisc / Punchstock

Acknowledgements

As usual, a work such as this would not have been possible without many people who have given their time and help to the author. Therefore, I would like to first thank those people who have and still do assist me in my academic endeavours, Professor David Hillier and David Smith, both of the University of Glamorgan, who are dependable and generous with their valuable insights and advice.

To the staff at the Police Division at Oxford University Press for their belief and support, and in particular to Lindsey Davis, who has kept me on the straight and narrow with her support and advice. Also, to all the staff at the Centre for Police Sciences at the University of Glamorgan for putting up with me!

I am indebted also to the Association of Police Authorities (APA) for their kindness in allowing me to use their map of Police Authority areas in England and Wales. A similar thank you must be registered to the anonymous reviewers who assisted in the process of putting the book proposal together.

Finally, to Alison and Alice, once again many thanks for sacrificing our time together to allow this work to be written and for continually supporting me in my endeavours.

Contents

Part One A Framework for Leading the Police

Part Two Supporting Leadership

Part Three Practical Leadership

List of Figures

List of Tables

Table of Statutes

Table of Statutory Instruments and Codes of Practice

A Framework for Leading the Police

Introduction to Leadership

1.1 **Introduction**

> The final test of a leader is that he (sic) leaves behind him in other men
> the conviction and the will to carry on.
>
> Lippmann (1945)

The quote from Walter Lippmann above highlights a major part of what leadership entails. The ability to inspire others to carry on with work once we have moved on or are not there to lead ourselves is a skill that many of us have to work hard to acquire. Being a leader is not as easy as it sounds. Sometimes a leader has to make unpopular decisions for the good of all. How this is achieved is also a skill that good leaders display. However, the work involved in the police service requires, on many occasions, for the constable or community support officer, to lead others at the scene of a road traffic collision, or when conducting a search for a missing child. The community that the police work with look to members of the police organization to lead them in a variety of ways and this means that leadership therefore is not confined to those who have specific ranks. What we also have to remember is, in line with the reform that surrounds the police and other public organizations, there is a flattening of management structures which means that people have to take more personal responsibility for their own work and that of others they work with.

It is not just a cliché that 'every officer is a leader'.

Being a leader means that your working life is different from others. It is just as well at this stage to think about what factors may change in your working life by being a leader. With this in mind try Exercise 1A below.

EXERCISE 1A

Write down the changes that being a leader may mean for you in the workplace.

Being a leader means that many areas of the way you work as an individual will be changed. For example you may have considered some of the following when trying Exercise 1A above.

- Looking after your own time.
- Colleagues and how being a leader affects your relationship with them.
- The things you have to do in work.
- Your relationship with other leaders in the police organization.

Clearly being a leader, whether leading people as a Sergeant or Inspector or at the scene of an incident or as part of a team is expected of police staff. Further, in an ideal world leaders would work within the parameters of clearly defined tasks, objectives, and different roles which would make life a lot easier. However, the reality is that this type of working environment is rare, especially within the police organization and its work; there is always ambiguity, inconsistency, and just the plain unknown that could occur at any time. This variety of work and having to deal with it spontaneously is one of the reasons why many people become police officers in the first place.

1.2 **Why is Leadership Important?**

The police service is a strange occupation in many ways. Not only does it have to deal with many different types of incidents and occurrences it encounters, but everyone within the service knows that they are expected by the public to have leadership qualities. This means that not just supervisors or management teams have to display skills and knowledge in leading others but that everyone, regardless of rank or role, must have leadership skills. This includes not only regular police officers, but Community Support Officers as well as the Special Constabulary and police staff. The reason why leadership is so important to the police service is linked to the aims and objectives of the job. Society demands the highest standards of behaviour and integrity from its police officers, as they strive to prevent crime and disorder, uphold the law, and protect the rights of citizens. Leadership is a key factor in the performance of the police and it plays a major role within the reform programme currently being undertaken. The public expects every member of the police to be decisive and to provide guidance and direction. Think of what you would do as a representative of the police and try the exercise below.

EXERCISE 1B

You have been asked to speak to a group representing your community about local parking problems outside a school.

This type of scenario is quite common for police officers and community support officers as part of the wider expectations of community consultation. Perhaps you would have thought of some of the following:

- Preparation of statistics relating to the problem in question.
- Inviting others along such as road safety and the school representatives to participate.
- Some options for resolving the problems.

Whatever your preparations, you would be expected by the meeting to *lead* the discussion, control the contributions of others and also bring the meeting to a successful conclusion. These are important leadership skills and are discussed in more depth within this book.

Research by the Home Office (Home Office 2004) has indicated that leadership in the police service has wide variations, including those individuals who were unethical, disinterested, or who failed to deal with poor performers. The same report, however, highlighted much common ground in terms of behaviour that was viewed by people as being good leadership.

1.3 What is Meant by Leadership?

When we talk of leadership what exactly do we mean? It appears be one of those qualities that you know when you see it, but is difficult to describe. There are almost as many definitions as there are commentators. Many link leadership with one person leading. Several points are worth mentioning here.

- To lead involves influencing others.
- Where there are leaders there are followers.
- Leaders seem to come to the fore when there is a crisis or special problem. In other words, they often become visible when an innovative response is needed.
- Leaders are people who have a clear idea of what they want to achieve and why.

We can see, therefore, that leaders are people who are able to think and act creatively in non-routine situations—and who set out to influence the actions, beliefs, and feelings of others. In this sense being a 'leader' is personal. It flows from an individual's qualities and actions. However, it is also often linked to some other role such as manager or expert. Here there can be a lot of confusion. Not all managers, for example, are leaders; and not all leaders are managers.

1.4 Some Basic Leadership Theories

In the recent literature of leadership (that is over the last 80 years or so) there have been four main areas of theory:

- Trait theories.
- Behavioural theories.
- Contingency theories.
- Transformational theories.

Van Maurik (2001), however, points out that each of these theories is not mutually exclusive of the others and that they are not constrained by the times in which they were considered popular. Therefore they could interact with each other and leaders may display attributes of some or all of these themes.

This typology of 'modern' approaches to leadership is sometimes understood by different titles (eg we might discuss charismatic rather than transformational leadership), and there are other possible candidates eg skill-based approaches and self-management or shared leadership. However, these four areas can be seen as sharing some common qualities—and we can approach them as variations of the 'classical' model of leadership.

1.4.1 **Traits**

Bennis (1998) highlights the fact that leaders are people, who are able to express themselves fully. 'They also know what they want', he continues, 'why they want it, and how to communicate what they want to others, in order to gain their co-operation and support.' Lastly, 'they know how to achieve their goals' (Bennis 1998: 3). But what is it that makes someone exceptional in this respect? As soon as we study the lives of people who have been labelled as great or effective leaders, it becomes clear that they have very different qualities. We only have to think of political figures like Nelson Mandela, Margaret Thatcher, and Mao Zedong to confirm this.

Instead of starting with exceptional individuals many turned to setting out the general qualities or *traits* they believed should be present. Surveys of early trait research by Stogdill (1948) and Mann (1959) reported that many studies identified personality characteristics that appear to differentiate leaders from followers. However, as Peter Wright (1996: 34) has commented, 'others found no differences between leaders and followers with respect to these characteristics, or even found people who possessed them were less likely to become leaders'. Yet pick up almost any of the popular books on the subject today and you will still find a list of traits that are thought to be central to effective leadership. The basic idea remains that if a person possesses these she or he will be able to take the lead in very different situations. At first glance, the lists seem to be helpful (see the Key Point box below).

KEY POINT—ATTRIBUTES OF A LEADER

John Gardner studied a large number of North American organizations and leaders and came to the conclusion that there were some qualities or attributes that appeared to show that a leader in one situation could lead in another. These included:

- physical vitality and stamina
- intelligence and action-oriented judgement
- eagerness to accept responsibility
- task competence
- an understanding of followers and their needs
- skill in dealing with people
- need for achievement
- capacity to motivate people
- courage and resolution
- trustworthiness
- decisiveness
- self-confidence
- assertiveness
- adaptability/flexibility.

(Gardner 1989)

The first problem is that early research into traits often assumed that there was a definite set of characteristics that made a leader—whatever the situation. In other words, they thought the same traits would work on a battlefield and in the board room of a business. They played down the impact of the situation the leader found themselves in at the time (Sadler 1997). They, and later writers, also tended to mix some very different qualities. Some of Gardner's qualities, for example, are aspects of a person's behaviour, some are skills, and others are to do with temperament and intellectual ability. Like other lists of this nature it is quite long—so what happens when someone has some but not all of the qualities? On the other hand, the list is not exhaustive and it is possible that someone might have other 'leadership qualities'.

More recently people have tried looking at what combinations of traits might be good for a particular situation. There is some mileage in this. It appears possible to link clusters of personality traits to success in different situations, as Stogdill has subsequently suggested (Wright 1996: 35).

One of the questions we hear most often around such lists concerns their apparent 'maleness' (eg Rosener 1997). When men and women are asked about each other's characteristics and leadership qualities, some significant patterns emerge. Both tend to have difficulties in seeing women as leaders. The attributes associated with leadership on these lists are often viewed as male. However, whether the characteristics of leaders can be gendered is questionable. If it is next to impossible to make a list of leadership traits that stands up to questioning, then the same certainly applies to lists of gender specific leadership traits.

1.4.2 Behaviours

As the search for trait theories lost ground, theorists turned to what leaders did—how they behaved. They moved from leaders to leadership—and this became the main way of approaching leadership within organizations in the 1950s and early 1960s. Different patterns of behaviour were grouped together and labelled as styles. This became a very popular activity within management training—perhaps the best known being Blake and Mouton's Managerial Grid (1964; 1978). Various schemes appeared, designed to diagnose and develop people's style of working. Despite different names, the basic ideas were very similar. The four main styles that appear are:

- **Concern for task.** Here leaders emphasize the achievement of concrete objectives. They look for high levels of productivity, and ways to organize people and activities in order to meet those objectives.
- **Concern for people.** In this style, leaders look upon their followers as people—their needs, interests, problems, development, and so on. They are not simply units of production or means to an end.
- **Directive leadership.** This style is characterized by leaders taking decisions for others—and expecting followers or subordinates to follow instructions.

- **Participative leadership.** Here leaders try to share decision-making with others (Wright 1996: 36–7).

Often, we find two of these styles present in books and training materials. For example, concern for task is set against concern for people (after Blake and Mouton 1964); and directive is contrasted with participative leadership (eg McGregor's (1960) portrayal of managers as 'Theory X' or 'Theory Y'). If you have been on a teamwork or leadership development course then it is likely you will have come across some variant of this in an exercise or discussion.

Many of the early writers that looked to participative and people-centred leadership, argued that it brought about greater satisfaction amongst followers (subordinates). However, as Sadler (1997) reports, when researchers really got to work on this it didn't seem to stand up. There were lots of differences and inconsistencies between studies. It was difficult to say style of leadership was significant in enabling one group to work better than another. Perhaps the main problem, though, was one shared with those who looked for traits (Wright 1996: 47). The researchers did not look properly at the context or setting in which the style was used. Is it possible that the same style would work as well in a gang or group of friends, as in a hospital emergency room? The styles that leaders can adopt are far more affected by those they are working with, and the environment they are operating within, than had been originally thought.

1.4.3 **Situations**

Researchers began to turn to the contexts in which leadership is exercised—and the idea that what is needed changes from situation to situation. Some looked to the processes by which leaders emerge in different circumstances—for example at moments of great crisis or where there is a vacuum. Others turned to the ways in which leaders and followers viewed each other in various contexts—for example in the army, political parties, and in companies. The most extreme view was that just about everything was determined by the context. But most writers did not take this route. They brought the idea of style with them, believing that the style needed would change with the situation. Another way of putting this is that particular contexts would demand particular forms of leadership. This placed a premium on people who were able to develop an ability to work in different ways, and could change their style to suit the situation.

What began to develop was a *contingency* approach. The central idea was that effective leadership was dependent on a mix of factors. For example, Fiedler argued that effectiveness depends on two interacting factors: leadership style, and the degree to which the situation gives the leader control and influence. Three things are important here:

- **The relationship between the leaders and followers.** If leaders are liked and respected they are more likely to have the support of others.

- **The structure of the task.** If the task is clearly spelled out as to goals, methods, and standards of performance then it is more likely that leaders will be able to exert influence.
- **Position power.** If an organization or group confers powers on the leader for the purpose of getting the job done, then this may well increase the influence of the leader (Fiedler and Garcia 1987: 51–67. See also Fiedler 1997).

Models like this can help us to think about what we are doing in different situations. For example, we may be more decisive where a quick response is needed, and where people are used to being told what to do, rather than having to work at it themselves. They also found their way into various management training aids—such as the development of Mouton and Blake's work by Reddin (1970; 1987) that looked to the interaction of the characteristics of the leader, the characteristics of the followers, and the situation; and Hersey and Blanchard's (1977) very influential discussion of choosing the appropriate style for the particular situation.

KEY POINT—HERSEY AND BLANCHARD (1977) ON LEADERSHIP STYLE AND SITUATION

Hersey and Blanchard identified four different leadership styles that could be drawn upon to deal with contrasting situations:

Telling (high task/low relationship behaviour). This style or approach is characterized by giving a great deal of direction to subordinates and by giving considerable attention to defining roles and goals. The style was recommended for dealing with new staff, or where the work was menial or repetitive, or where things had to be completed within a short time span. Subordinates are viewed as being unable and unwilling to 'do a good job'.

Selling (high task/high relationship behaviour). Here, while most of the direction is given by the leader, there is an attempt at encouraging people to 'buy into' the task. Sometimes characterized as a 'coaching' approach, it is to be used when people are willing and motivated but lack the required 'maturity' or 'ability'.

Participating (high relationship/low task behaviour). Here decision-making is shared between leaders and followers—the main role of the leader being to facilitate and communicate. It entails high support and low direction and is used when people are able, but are perhaps unwilling or insecure (they are of 'moderate to high maturity').

Delegating (low relationship/low task behaviour). The leader still identifies the problem or issue, but the responsibility for carrying out the response is given to followers. It entails having a high degree of competence and maturity (people know what to do, and are motivated to do it).

(Hersey 1984)

Aside from their very general nature, there are some issues with such models. First, much that has been written has a North American bias. There is a lot of evidence to suggest cultural factors influence the way that people carry out, and respond to, different leadership styles. For example, some cultures are more individualistic, or value family as against bureaucratic models, or have very different expectations about how people address and talk with each other. All this impacts on the choice of style and approach.

Secondly, as we saw earlier, there may be different patterns of leadership linked with men and women. Some have argued that women may have leadership styles that are more nurturing, caring, and sensitive. They look more to relationships. Men are said to look to the task. However, there is a lot of debate about this. We can find plenty of examples of nurturing men and task-oriented women. Any contrasts between the style of men and women may be down to the situation. In management, for example, women are more likely to be in positions of authority in people-oriented sectors—so this aspect of style is likely to be emphasized.

Thirdly, as Bolman and Deal (1997: 302) comment, like Blake and Mouton before them, writers like Hersey and Blanchard 'focus mainly on the relationship between managers and immediate subordinates, and say little about issues of structure, politics or symbols'.

1.5 Transactional and Transformational Leadership for Police

We live in an increasingly diverse and complicated society. This has an impact upon the police service and the way in which it is run, attempts to achieve its objectives and deals with the people that work for it. Globalization, the increase in transnational crime, cross border criminal activity, and the local commitment of the police service mean that there are high levels of uncertainty for everyone.

Consequently, there is a need for individuals who are stable in an emotional sense, and who are competent in the skills and knowledge required for good leadership.

In order for police leaders to perform their tasks to a high level of performance, there is a need to understand the two approaches that currently underpin the way police leadership is taught within the police organization. These are Transactional and Transformational leadership approaches.

1.5.1 Transactional leadership

This approach to being a leader has been linked to the use of negotiation, promise, and bargaining between the leader and those he/she is supposed to be leading. It is not interested in moral development of the individual being lead, but merely with achieving a particular task or end result. In some senses it involves the leader supplying what the followers want or think they want and they in turn provide what the leader wants. However, the people involved in the bargain have no long-term reasons for holding them together, and consequently people involved in this approach tend to go their separate ways. There is no doubt that a leadership act took place, but it is not one that binds the leader and the follower together in a 'pursuit of a high purpose' (Burns 1978:19).

Definition—Transactional leadership

Transactional leadership, whilst being pragmatic, revolves around negotiation and bargaining between the leader and the followers to achieve a specific goal. It is task-oriented and does not include such skills as staff development.

1.5.2 **Transformational leadership**

Whilst transactional leadership tends to focus upon the task or the system in hand, transformational leaders tend to focus on the interpersonal, teams and people-centred approach. This approach is sometimes referred to as charismatic leadership. These individuals spend time and invest their effort in others, helping them improve their skills levels and generally supporting them in their day-to-day work tasks. The transformational approach focuses on the benefit for others, the requirements of the organization and is usually underpinned by honesty, integrity, and ethical approaches to carrying out their role.

Burns (1978) argued that it was possible to distinguish between transactional and transforming leaders. The former, 'approach their followers with an eye to trading one thing for another (1978: 4), while the latter are visionary leaders who seek to appeal to their follower's 'better nature and move them toward higher and more universal needs and purposes' (Bolman and Deal 1997: 314). In other words, the leader is seen as a change agent.

A comparison between transactional and transformational leadership

Transactional	Transformational
The transactional leader:	The transformational leader:
• Recognizes what it is that we want to get from work and tries to ensure that we get it if our performance merits it.	• Raises our level of awareness, our level of consciousness about the significance and value of designated outcomes, and ways of reaching them.
• Exchanges rewards and promises for our effort. Is responsive to our immediate self-interests if they can be met by getting the work done.	• Gets us to rise above our own self-interest for the sake of the team, organization, or larger policy needs.
	• Alters our needs and expands our range of wants and needs.

Source: Based on Bass 1985—Wright 1996: 213.

Bass (1985) was concerned that Burns (1978) set transactional and transforming leaders as polar opposites. Instead, he suggests we should be looking at the way in which transactional forms can be drawn upon and transformed. The resulting transformational leadership is said to be necessary because of the more sophisticated demands made of leaders. Van Maurik (2001: 75) argues that such demands 'centre around the high levels of uncertainty experienced by leaders, their staff and, indeed, the whole organization . . . today'. He goes on to identify three broad bodies of writers in this orientation. Those concerned with:

- Team leadership, eg Meredith Belbin.
- The leader as a catalyst of change, eg Warren Bennis, James Kouzes and Barry Posner, and Stephen R. Covey.
- The leader as a strategic visionary eg Peter Senge

The dividing lines between these is a matter for some debate; the sophistication of the analysis offered by different writer's understanding; and some of the writers may not recognize their placement—but there would appear to be a body of material that can be labelled transformational. There is strong emphasis in the contemporary literature of management leadership on charismatic and related forms of leadership. However, whether there is a solid body of evidence to support its effectiveness is an open question. Indeed, Wright (1996: 221) concludes 'it is impossible to say how effective transformational leadership is with any degree of certainty'.

1.5.3 Reflecting upon a combined approach

A good leader utilizes many approaches and there is now a drive to produce leaders within the police service as being focused and competent in addressing transnational tasks and activities whilst doing so in a transformational way. For example, being task-centred in your leadership approach may be efficient in the short term, but may have detrimental consequences in the long term. Similarly, being particularly people-centred could mean that people will like you but that the important tasks that you have to achieve will not get done. With the information provided so far in this chapter, try the following two exercises.

EXERCISE 1C Your leadership style

Using the information provided so far in this chapter, reflect upon your personal leadership style. Write down on a piece of paper which style you believe suits you and provide supporting reasons for your view.

EXERCISE 1D Skills required of a leader

Construct a table indicating how you think you measure up to what is required for the role of a leader and the responsibilities that go along with it. Indicate a score of 1 to 5 with 1 being the weakest and 5 being the strongest, alongside the skills you have identified.

For example if you think your communication skills are excellent give yourself a 5. If they are not very good you should give yourself a 1 or 2. Once you have highlighted any perceived weaknesses, show what you can do to improve them.

Skills required of a Leader	How I score	What can I do to improve
Communication skills	2	Practice my writing and delivery skils. Become more engaged in classroom discussion.

1.6 Police Reform and its Challenges for Police Leaders

Those in the police service who aspire to be good leaders must acknowledge the significant amount of change and reform that has taken place, and will continue to take place, for the foreseeable future. This knowledge is vitally important if a leader is to understand the changes and lead their staff through potentially difficult times as individuals adjust to the changes brought about by the reform programme.

The police reform programme is a series of changes instituted by the present government after the 2001 general election. Signalled by the White Paper, *Policing a New Century: a Blueprint for Reform*, it has so far included the establishment of the Police Standards Unit, the introduction of the Police Reform Act 2002, and the introduction of the National Policing Plan. The reform programme has far-reaching implications for the police service and will greatly influence both managers and leaders within it. As such, police leaders need to understand the background of the police reform programme and several areas that will influence them.

1.6.1 **The Police Reform Act 2002**

The overall intention of the Police Reform Act 2002 is highlighted in the Key Point box below:

KEY POINT—THE INTENTION OF THE POLICE REFORM ACT 2002

An Act to make provision about the supervision, administration, functions and conduct of police forces, police officers and other persons serving with, or carrying out functions in relation to the police: to amend police powers and to provide for the exercise of police powers by persons who are not police officers; to amend the law relating to anti social-behaviour orders; to amend the law relating to sex offenders; and for connected purposes [Long title of the Police Reform Act].

(Home Office 2002)

The Police Reform Act 2002 is one of the most important Acts of Parliament regarding the police and policing in England and Wales in modern times. It forms the backbone of the government's agenda for reforming the police service in England and Wales and received Royal Assent on 24 July 2002. The provisions of the Act are being brought about in stages by a series of commencement orders, thus allowing the government to implement certain parts of the Act when it sees fit. The main provisions of the Act can be summarized as follows:

1.6.2 **The National Policing Plan**

The National Policing Plan sets out the government's strategy for policing over the coming years and police authorities are required to also produce a three-year strategy plan which is supposed to be consistent with the National Policing Plan. The usual key priorities of the National Policing Plan are to reduce overall crime (including violent and drug-related crime); provide a citizen-focused police service; in partnership with others, to increase detection rates and target prolific offenders; reduce people's concerns about crime, disorder and anti-social behaviour, and combat serious and organized crime. The current National Policing Plan covering the years 2006 to 2009 is incorporated within the National Community Safety Plan 2006–2009.

1.6.3 **Inefficiency**

It provides powers to make a police force remedy any problems of inefficiency and ineffectiveness highlighted by Her Majesty's Inspector of Constabulary (HMIC). These powers enhance those already in being under section 40 of the Police Act 1996 which allows the Home Secretary to direct a police authority to take specific remedial action following an adverse report by HMIC. In particular the Police

Reform Act 2002 introduces a new power enabling the Secretary of State to direct a police authority to produce, in conjunction with the relevant chief officer, an action plan to address the poor performance highlighted by HMIC. It strengthens police authorities in that it enables them to require departure or suspension of a chief constable in the interest of the public.

1.6.4 **Community support officers**

The Police Reform Act introduced not only the familiar community support officers, but also allows for investigating officers, and detention and escort officers in order to help police officers to deal with low level crime and anti-social behaviour. This was initially proposed in *Policing a New Century: A Blueprint for Reform (2001)* and has three main functions:

- Freeing up officers' time for their core functions by making more effective use of these individuals.
- Employing more specialist investigating officers to provide expertise in combating specialist crime such as finance and information technology.
- Providing additional capacity to combat low level disorder, and thereby help reduce the public's fear of crime. In this way, the government proposes to harness the commitment of those already engaged in crime reduction activities such as traffic wardens, neighbourhood and street wardens, and security staff.

1.6.5 **Accreditation of others**

The Act also introduces the ability to accredit members of the extended policing family, for example street wardens. This means under certain circumstances, limited police powers can be granted to persons already engaged in community safety activities. It could also include individuals such as football stewards, as well as security guards within the private security industry. Even persons with official powers such as Environmental Health Officers may be included. Each relevant chief officer has discretion for conferring powers on accredited individuals, and they may also attach conditions and restrictions to the powers. Schedule 5 to the Police Reform Act 2002 lists a menu of powers that may be conferred upon accredited individuals.

The following bullet points show these powers:

- The power to issue fixed penalty notices.
- The power to require the giving of name and address.
- The power to require the name and address of a person acting in an antisocial manner.
- The power to prevent alcohol consumption in designated public places.
- The power to confiscate alcohol and tobacco.
- The power to remove abandoned vehicles.

1.7 **Other Important Areas**

The Police Reform Act 2002 also establishes independence in the investigation of complaints against the police by the introduction of the Independent Police Complaints Commission (see the Chapter on Ethical Policing later in this book). It modifies and introduces police powers including adding to the list of offences with a power to arrest, strengthening police powers when dealing with anti-social use of vehicles, and introducing interim orders for the Anti-Social Behaviour Order process. The Act provides powers to ensure the application of good practice across the country. This is being carried out by the Police Standards Unit.

1.7.1 **The Police Standards Unit**

The Police Standards Unit (PSU) was set up by the Home Office in July 2001 and is now considered a vital part of the government's police reform agenda. The main focus of the Unit's activities is to measure and compare Basic Command Unit (BCU) and local partnership performance. This means trying to understand underlying causes of performance variations, identifying and disseminating good practice, and providing support and advice to those who need it.

In order to achieve this, the PSU identifies BCUs' or forces' performances based on HMIC reports, statistical information, or cases of particular concern that have been highlighted. As part of his process, the Unit will engage with other agencies to ensure their effective contribution, and this includes crime and disorder partnerships.

Clearly the police reform programme supports the concept of community safety and crime reduction, widening access to the provision of police services, and involving communities at a much greater level than before, whilst ensuring the police provide a quality product which is both effective and efficient.

1.7.2 **Recent developments: 'Cutting Crime—A New Partnership 2008–11'**

In July 2007 the government produced a new strategic document entitled 'Cutting Crime—A New Partnership 2008–11', (Home Office 2007). This document builds on the previous 10 years of police activity in tackling crime and disorder. However, one of the important aspects of this document is the decline of central government control and direction in terms of tackling crime and disorder and the increase of local community involvement in the process. The implications for the police leader are quite significant in that the local delivery will mean enhanced leadership and decision-making skills will be required at a local level in the delivery of services based on local consultation rather than being directed from the centre.

1.8 **Summing Up**

1.8.1 **The importance of leadership**

Society demands the highest standards of behaviour and integrity from its police officers, as they strive to prevent crime and disorder, uphold the law, and protect the rights of citizens. Leadership is a key factor in the performance of the police and it plays a major role within the reform programme currently being undertaken. The public expects every member of the police to be decisive and to provide guidance and direction.

1.8.2 **Types of leadership**

There are some basic ideas about what component parts make up a leader. These include:

- To lead involves influencing others.
- Where there are leaders there are followers.
- Leaders seem to come to the fore when there is a crisis or special problem. In other words, they often become visible when an innovative response is needed.
- Leaders are people who have a clear idea of what they want to achieve and why.

There have been four main areas of theory concerning what makes a leader. These basic ideas revolve around:

- Trait theories.
- Behavioural theories.
- Contingency theories.
- Transformational theories.

1.8.3 **Transactional leadership**

It has been said that transactional leadership, whilst being pragmatic, revolves around negotiation and bargaining between the leader and the followers to achieve a specific goal. It is task-oriented and does not include such skills as staff development.

1.8.4 **Transformational leadership**

Whilst transactional leadership tends to focus upon the task or the system in hand, transformational leaders tend to focus on the interpersonal, teams and people-centred approach. This approach is sometimes referred to as charismatic leadership.

1.8.5 **Police reform and its implications for leaders**

The police reform programme is a series of changes instituted by the present government after the 2001 general election. Signalled by the White Paper, *Policing a New Century: a Blueprint for Reform*, it has so far included the establishment of the PSU, the introduction of the Police Reform Act 2002, and the introduction of the National Policing Plan. The reform programme has far-reaching implications for the police service and will greatly influence both managers and leaders within it. As such, police leaders need to understand the background of the police reform programme and several areas that will influence them.

References and Further Reading

Lippmann, Walter (1945) as cited in Augarde T. (1992) *The Oxford Dictionary of Modern Quotations*, Oxford: Oxford University Press, 189, 1.

Bass, B.M. (1985) *Leadership and Performance Beyond Expectation*, New York: Free Press.

Bennis, W. (1998) *On Becoming a Leader*, London: Arrow.

Blake, R.R. and Mouton, J.S. (1964) *The Managerial Grid*, Houston TX. Gulf.

Blake, R.R. and Mouton, J.S. (1978) *The New Managerial Grid*, Houston TX. Gulf.

Bolman, L.G. and Deal, T.E. (1997) *Reframing Organizations: Artistry, Choice and Leadership*, Jossey Bass Wiley, USA.

Burns, J.M. (1978) *Leadership*, New York: HarperCollins.

Fiedler, F.E. and Garcia, J.E. (1987) *New Approaches to Effective Leadership*, New York: John Wiley.

Fiedler, F.E. (1997) 'Situational control and a dynamic theory of leadership' in K. Grint (ed.) (1997) *Leadership. Classical, Contemporary, and Critical Approaches*, Oxford: Oxford University Press.

Gardner, J. (1989) *On Leadership*, New York: Free Press.

Hersey, P. (1984) *The Situational Leader*, New York: Warner.

Hersey, P. and Blanchard, K.H. (1977) *The Management of Organizational Behaviour*, Upper Saddle River N.J.: Prentice Hall.

Home Office (2001) *Policing a New Century: A Blueprint for Reform*, London: Home Office.

Home Office (2002) *The Police Reform Act*, London: Home Office.

Home Office (2004) *Police Leadership: Expectations and Impact*, London: Home Office.

Home Office (2007) *Cutting Crime-A new Partnership 2008–11*, London: Home Office.

McGregor, D. (1960) *The Human Side of Enterprise*, New York: McGraw Hill.

Mann, R.D. (1959) 'A review of the relationship between personality and performance in small groups', *Psychological Bulletin* 66(4): 241–70.

Reddin, W.J. (1987) *How to Make Management Style More Effective*, Maidenhead: McGraw Hill.

Rosener, J.B. 'Sexual static' in K. Grint (ed.) (1997) *Leadership. Classical, Contemporary, and Critical Approaches*, Oxford: Oxford University Press.

Sadler, P. (1997) *Leadership*, Kogan Page, London.

Senge, P.M. (1990) *The Fifth Discipline. The Art and Practice of the Learning Organization*, London: Random House.

Stogdill, R.M. (1948) 'Personal factors associated with leadership. A survey of the literature', *Journal of Psychology* 25: 35–71.

Sun Tzu, (2005) *The Art of War*, Shambhala *Publications, USA.*

Van Maurik, J. (2001) *Writers on Leadership*, Penguin Books, London.

Wright, P. (1996) *Managerial Leadership*, London: Routledge.

Useful websites

The Home Office Police website available at <http://police.homeoffice.gov.uk/>.

The Police Standards Unit website available at <http://police.homeoffice.gov.uk/about-us/index.html/police-standards-unit/>.

The Police Reform Website available at <http://police.homeoffice.gov.uk/about-us/police-reform-resources-info/>.

SPACE FOR NOTES

SPACE FOR NOTES

SPACE FOR NOTES

Management Structures within the Police Service

2.1 **Introduction**

Any person who considers themselves a professional representative of the police service should have a sound knowledge of the basic management structure and supporting systems within the organization as a whole. As a leader you will need to understand the basic knowledge surrounding the introduction and functions of most of these as you may well have to explain these to others and utilize some of their functions to help you in your role. This chapter introduces and reinforces the knowledge surrounding the rank structure, typical force structures, important agencies such as the Association of Chief Police Officers (ACPO), the National Police Improvement Agency (NPIA), accountability, and governance systems as well as the Police Leadership Quality Framework. This information is important for leaders and potential managers alike, if they are to understand the organization within which they lead.

2.2 **Rank and Structure within the Police Service**

Police officers have a formal rank structure similar to that of the army. The insignia of the ranks in the Police Service are shown in Figure 2.1. The prefix 'detective' is used to denote specialist duties but it is not a rank in itself.

In London, officers of Assistant Chief Constable rank are known as Commanders. The most senior rank in the Metropolitan and City of London Police forces is that of Commissioner whereas in other forces the most senior rank is Chief Constable. Figure 2.1 below illustrates the rank and insignia of police officers.

Whilst most police forces take into account local circumstances and consultation which helps shape their force and their structure, Figure 2.2 illustrates the general or typical way in which a police force may be organized.

The Chief Constable is the most senior police officer and is ultimately responsible for the achievement of plans jointly agreed with the Police Authority.

Below the Chief Constable are the Deputy and Assistant Chief Constables. In addition to holding a specific portfolio, the Deputy Chief Constable deputizes for the Chief Constable as required.

The Assistant Chief Officer, in charge of budgeting and resources, is the chief administrative officer of the force. The post-holder is not usually a police officer and he or she will have responsibilities for large departments (Human Resources, Accounts, Estates, and Finance).

Below the senior management team are Basic Command units, each headed by a police officer of the rank of Chief Superintendent or Superintendent. The number of BCUs depends upon the size and population of the areas within the force. Each BCU may have five to 10 police stations, some operating 24 hours a day. The Specialist Divisions have different functions. For example, the Operational Support Division includes search teams, tactical operations and firearm teams, road policing, dogs, and helicopters. The Communications Division

Figure 2.1 Ranks and insignia of police officers

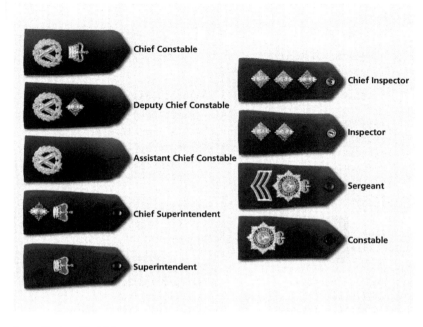

Source: Courtesy of Kent Police.

Figure 2.2 A typical organization of a medium to small-sized police force

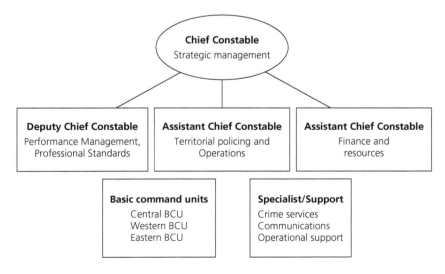

is responsible for the control rooms and call centres. Figure 2.3 shows the breakdown of a typical Basic Command Unit and of a Centralized Crime Division based at HQ.

Figure 2.3 A typical BCU structure

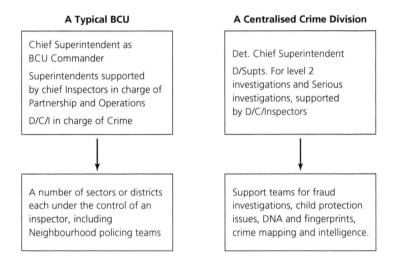

The larger the force, the greater the number of senior officers and territorial divisions and the wider the range of specialist divisions.

2.2.1 **The strength of the police service**

The strength of the police service is constantly monitored by the Home Office and figures are produced at intervals. At the time of writing (June 2007) the latest figures available for police service strength in England and Wales can be seen in Table 2.1. This figure does not include the British Transport Police, nor officers on central service secondments, nor Serious Organised Crime Agency staff.

Table 2.1 Police service strength in England and Wales as at 30 September 2006

Role	Total in Role
Police officers	139,486
Police staff	73,175
Community support officers	2194
Total	214,855

2.3 **Governance and Accountability**

Accountability becomes an issue when there is public concern that the arrangements for ensuring that the police perform their job satisfactorily do not appear to be working. This concern may arise because of apparent misuse of police powers or a wasteful use of resources or anything else that appears to threaten the obligations of the police to the society they serve. It is fair to say, however, that the police service in England and Wales is probably one of the most accountable organizations in the country. Constables are accountable to the courts for their actions, to the Crown Prosecution service for their cases, to the Police Code of Conduct and can be investigated by the Independent Police Complaints Committee. Chief Constables are constrained by Acts of Parliament and are accountable to Police Authorities for the management of their forces. Furthermore, the police are accountable to the communities they serve through a variety of consultation processes such as the Partnerships And Community Talking (PACT) programme.

In terms of structure the police service is managed by something called the tripartite system of control. This is made up of the chief officer of police for the police force in question, central government in the role of the Home Secretary, and the local police authority. In theory there is a balance between the three of these roles and it is this system which will be considered next.

2.3.1 **The tripartite system**

The formal structure of police governance in England and Wales is directed by that introduced under the Police Act of 1964 (Home Office 1964) and is commonly referred to as the tripartite system. This Act divided accountability for policing between the Chief Constable, local police authorities, and the Home Secretary, based in the Home Office. Figure 2.4 below illustrates the tripartite system.

Figure 2.4 The tripartite system of accountability of the police in England and Wales

Each of the three roles will be discussed briefly.

2.3.2 **The role of the Chief Constable**

In general the Chief Constable of a police force is invested with the power of direction and control of his/her force for they have the power to appoint, promote, and discipline all staff up to Chief Superintendent level and to investigate complaints against the police.

Further the Chief Constable has overall responsibility for the production of force annual policing plans involving locally agreed targets with the community and also for overseeing an agreed budget in order to achieve these agreed aims and for other policing functions.

2.3.3 **The role of the Police Authority**

A Police Authority is an independent body made up of local people. The Police Authority's job is to make sure that the community has an efficient and effective local police force. There is a police authority for each local police force—43 in all in England and Wales—plus an additional one for British Transport Police. In Northern Ireland the Police Authority is called the Policing Board but it has a similar role to Police Authorities in England and Wales.

All Police Authorities are members of the Association of Police Authorities.

Most Police Authorities have 17 members namely:

- nine local councillors appointed by the local council;
- five independent members selected following local advertisements;
- three magistrates from the local area.

The Metropolitan Police Authority has 23 members because of London's size.

The main job of the Police Authority is to set the strategic direction for the force and holds the Chief Constable to account on behalf of the local community. Delivering policing services is the job of the Chief Constable.

In short, the Police Authority:

- Holds the police budget and decides how much council tax should be raised for policing.
- Appoints (and dismisses) the Chief Constable and senior police officers.
- Consults widely with local people to find out what they want from their local police.
- Sets local policing priorities based on the concerns of local people and targets for achievement.
- Monitors everything the police do and how well they perform against the targets set by the authority.
- Publishes a three-year plan and an annual plan which tells local people what they can expect from their police service and reports back at the end of the year.
- Makes sure local people get best value from their local police force.
- Oversees complaints against the police and disciplines senior officers.

The main function of a Police Authority therefore is to make sure that the local police are accountable for what they do within the community—that is the people who live or work in the area—and that they have a say in how they are policed.

Figure 2.5 below illustrates the geographic location of the police authorities in England and Wales.

Figure 2.5 The geographic location of the police authorities in England and Wales

Source: Adapted with permission from the APA website available at:
<http://www.apa.police.uk/APA/About+Police+Authorities/National+Map/>

It is the Police Authority that controls the size of the budget and which is ultimately responsible for maintaining an efficient and effective police force. The Police Authority consists of 17 local councillors, magistrates, and independent members and it is mainly through these members that the police service is accountable to the population at large. The responsibilities of the Chief Constable and Police Authority are shown in Table 2.2 below.

Table 2.2 Responsibilities of chief constables and police authorities

Chief constable	Police authority
In overall command of the force and holds ultimate responsibility for operational matters.	Holds ultimate responsibility for the efficiency and effectiveness of the force.
Drafts local plans for Basic Command Units (BCUs).	Sets overall budget and approves any additional expenditure.
Responsible for achieving local force goals.	Drafts local plans and goals for local forces. Drafts three-year force strategy in accordance with National Police Plan.
Has control of expenditure within an agreed budget.	
	Consults with local population.

2.3.4 **The role of the Home Office**

The third part of the tripartite organization of the police is the Home Office, which is very influential in directing the work of the police service, often using specially earmarked funds to bring about improvements in crime reduction. The Home Office is a department of central government and its priorities are those of the political party in power in Westminster. Government legislation now defines the overall priorities of the police service, many of its methods of working and even the ways in which the success of individual police forces are measured. Having discussed the structure of the police service, the next section will introduce the general system in use for the promotion of police officers.

2.4 **The General System of Promotion**

The current promotion system in use throughout the police service in England and Wales relies upon qualifying examinations known as the OSPRE system. This system is divided into two distinct and separate parts, namely Part 1 and Part 2.

2.4.1 **Part 1 OSPRE**

Part 1 for the Sergeants' and Inspectors' examinations consists of a single, multiple choice paper of three hours' length, consisting of 150 questions. The syllabus is divided into four specific categories namely:

- Crime
- Evidence and procedure
- Road traffic
- General police duties.

The syllabus content that is subject to examination is contained within the latest editions of *Blackstone's Police Manuals* and candidates for promotion are normally examined on the law and procedure as it appears in the latest editions of this publication.

The content of each subject is identified as a result of a nationwide survey of operational sergeants and inspectors, together with a strategic input from the police service. From this, areas of the syllabus that are of importance and frequently encountered by officers form the basic template for the examination. This means that potential officers of the rank of sergeants and inspectors will be tested in areas that have been identified as the most relevant and frequently encountered by officers already serving in the rank. Whilst there will inevitably be similarities for both ranks, there will be some rank specific areas. For example, sergeants are expected to know, at a basic level, the responsibilities of Inspectors and Superintendents under the Police and Criminal Evidence Act 1984 (Home Office 1984). Inspectors would expect to have a higher level of knowledge in this area. However, whilst candidates are expected to have a high level of knowledge they are not normally tested on their ability to simply recall information that is contained solely within the text of the manuals.

2.4.2 Part 2 OSPRE

Part 2 of OSPRE contains exercises which have been designed from information derived from job analysis of the rank which the candidate aspires to attain. These are normally tested under the assessment centre design principles.

Information provided to candidates in the assessment centres tends to be in the form of a job description, ie commentating on a letter/report, dealing with a staff issue or a complaint from a member of the public, whilst the competencies which define the behaviour expected whilst dealing with the issue are examined. As can be seen, the job description and the competencies are vital for this process.

The competencies that are tested are to be found in the Integrated Competency Framework. The framework contains three parts of information associated with each rank/role: Tasks, Knowledge, and Behaviours and all this information is contained within what is referred to as the Rank/Role Profile.

The task content of the profile is very similar to the tasks and responsibilities contained in a job description. This highlights clearly what the post-holder is supposed to do. The knowledge content highlights the areas of the law and procedures the post-holder has to use to function effectively in that particular job.

There are 12 behavioural competencies in total. Each one has a title, an overall definition and has one, two, or three levels. The general Behavioural Competency areas can be seen in Table 2.3 below.

Table 2.3 The competency behavioural framework

Behavioural competency area

1. Community and customer focus
2. Effective communication
3. Maximizing potential
4. Negotiation and influencing
5. Openness to change
6. Personal responsibility
7. Planning and organizing
8. Problem solving
9. Resilience
10. Respect for race and diversity
11. Strategic perspective
12. Team working

Since the Inspectors Part 2 assessment centre in 2004, candidates have been assessed against the competencies set out in the Integrated Competency Framework and only those listed will now be assessed.

2.5 Other Important Police Groups

It is not just the rank structure or the hierarchy and organizational style of a police force that determines how it is led. There are other very important police groups that influence and advise the police on policy and structure, and importantly, on performance management, diversity, and other matters that the police leader should be aware of. This section examines the major groups or organizations that leaders should know about.

2.5 1 The Association of Chief Police Officers

The Association of Chief Police Officers (ACPO) is an independent, professionally led strategic body in an equal and active partnership with government and the Association of Police Authorities. ACPO leads and coordinates the direction and development of the police service in England, Wales, and Northern Ireland. In times of national need ACPO—on behalf of all chief officers—coordinates the strategic policing response.

ACPO is not a staff association as may be commonly understood (the separately constituted Chief Police Officers' Association fulfils that function). ACPO's work is on behalf of the service, rather than its own members and has the status of a private company limited by guarantee. As such, it conforms to the requirements of company law and its affairs are governed by a board of directors. It is funded by a combination of a Home Office grant, contributions from each of the Police Authorities, membership subscriptions, and by the proceeds of its annual exhibition. ACPO's members are police officers who hold the rank of Chief Constable, Deputy Chief Constable or Assistant Chief Constable, or their equivalents. They represent all the forces of England, Wales and Northern Ireland, national police agencies, and certain other forces in the UK, the Isle of Man, and the Channel Islands, and certain senior non-police staff. There are presently 280 members of ACPO.

2.5.2 The Association of Police Authorities

The Association of Police Authorities (APA) was set up on 1 April 1997 to represent Police Authorities in England, Wales, and Northern Ireland, both on the national stage and locally. It influences policy on policing and it supports local Police Authorities in their important role, and as such the APA is the national voice of local Police Authorities.

The APA is funded by subscriptions from member authorities and has two main roles to perform. These are:

• to act as the national voice of all police authorities; and
• to help police authorities in doing their job locally.

The APA hopes to achieve this by its specific aims which are to:

• influence the national policing agenda on behalf of Police Authorities and local communities;
• promote awareness of policing needs and the role and achievements of Police Authorities;
• support Police Authorities in securing efficient and effective policing services across the country;
• help Police Authorities improve how they do their job; and
• uphold and champion the principles of local accountability and policing by consent.

The APA works closely with its member authorities and partners to:

• develop APA policies on all national policing, criminal justice, and community safety related issues;
• raise public awareness of Police Authority concerns;
• lobby government and others to ensure that the views of local Police Authorities and their communities influence the national policing agenda;
• keep local Police Authorities up to date with current national developments;

- develop guidance and advice to assist authorities in carrying out their role locally; and
- identify and spread good practice through conferences, seminars and training workshops, research, and publications.

2.5.3 Her Majesty's Inspectors of Constabulary

For over 150 years Her Majesty's Inspectors of Constabulary (HMIC) have been charged with examining and improving the efficiency of the police service in England and Wales (and latterly Northern Ireland), with the first HMIC appointed under the provisions of the County and Borough Police Act 1856.

HMICs are appointed by the Crown on the recommendation of the Home Secretary and report to Her Majesty's Chief Inspector of Constabulary (HMCIC), who is the Home Secretary's principal professional policing adviser. The HMCIC is independent both of the Home Office and of the police service.

The first HMICs were appointed under the provisions of the County and Borough Police Act 1856. In 1962, the Royal Commission on the Police formally acknowledged their contribution to policing. The statutory duties of HMIC are described in the Police Act 1996 (Home Office 1996).

In addition, the Home Secretary lays before Parliament a clear statement of the duties and responsibilities which the Inspectorate is expected to fulfil.

In October 1993, and in accordance with the Citizen's Charter principle that Inspectorates should include a 'lay element', two HMIC were appointed from non-police backgrounds. This development underlined the Inspectorate's commitment to objectivity, independence, and openness. It also broadened and enhanced its professional base by introducing top management experience from commercial and industrial organizations. This has since been taken forward with the appointment of two HMIC from non-police backgrounds (one specializing in police training) and an Assistant Inspector for Community and Race Relations.

More generally, the work of the Inspectorate reinforces the principles of public service set out in the Citizen's Charter which is shown in the Key Point box below.

KEY POINT—STATEMENT OF PURPOSE

To promote the efficiency and effectiveness of policing in England, Wales, and Northern Ireland through inspection of police organizations and functions to ensure:

1. agreed standards are achieved and maintained;
2. good practice is spread; and
3. performance is improved.

(continued)

> Also, to provide advice and support to the tripartite partners (Home Secretary, Police Authorities and forces) and play an important role in *the development of future leaders.*

Inspections and assessments

The formal inspection process has long been a core Inspectorate activity, through which HMIC conduct detailed examinations of those areas of policing organization and practice judged to be central to the efficient and effective discharge of the policing function.

Baseline inspections

A new methodology, Baseline Assessment, has been introduced by HMIC. HMIC has long kept its methodology for inspection under review. In 2002 HMIC identified a need to rethink the conventional formal inspection methodology used at force level in the light of the police reform programme: new business in the form of efficiency plans; Best Value Reviews and Basic Command Unit inspections; comprehensive performance assessments; and pressures to undertake more cross-cutting work across the Criminal Justice System as drivers for change.

Of these, perhaps the most pressing was the impact of the police reform programme and the broad thrust of the reform initiative are on the whole supported by the whole service. Although HMIC is an independent inspectorate, and not a Home Office policy unit, they are considered a lead player in many of the key discussions and appear committed to the scale and nature of the improvements which the reforms will promote.

HMIC's approach of bringing together a range of quantitative and qualitative information and judgments allow them to compile a comprehensive assessment of each force, the Baseline Assessment. This generates a bespoke, three-year review programme for each force, with areas of critical weakness or under-performance being made subject to a focused inspection. A key point is that this programme is synchronized with the force's own assessment of where its strengths and weaknesses lie, and its proposals for tackling the latter. Where a force is performing well, the inspection activity is simply to analyse, learn, and disseminate good practice. Where a force has a sound action plan to improve an area of under-performance, the inspection activity may simply be to keep a watching brief, unless HMIC's help is requested. The Baseline Assessment thus promotes what can be seen as a shared agenda for improvement. The first Baseline Assessment reports were published in 2004 and are published annually each October.

2.5.4 The National Police Improvement Agency

Together with its partners ACPO, APA, and the Home Office the National Police Improvement Agency (NPIA) support forces in order to deliver the best possible policing services to the public.

The agency hopes to provide leadership and expertise to the service in areas as diverse as information and communications technology, support to information and intelligence sharing, core police processes, managing change, and recruiting, developing, and deploying people.

As a single national organization the aim of the NPIA is to streamline and simplify the way policing improvement is delivered locally and nationally.

They will be responsible for delivering and improving the critical support those police officers rely on to do their jobs, including:

- National information systems such as the Police National Computer, National DNA Database and IDENT1, the national fingerprint and palm print system.
- Specialist training for high-tech crime, forensics, and major investigations.
- Clear and secure voice communication through the Airwave service.
- Round-the-clock specialist operational policing advice to guide forces through murder investigations, public order events, major incidents, and searches.
- National development programmes to nurture the next generation of police officers at all levels from PC to the senior ranks.

In addition, the NPIA will work towards improvements in the following areas:

- Intelligence, information and interoperability.
- Publish a National Strategic Assessment, produced to a new, agreed standard.
- Resource, re-profile and deliver the IMPACT Programme.
- Support the ACPO crime and counter-terrorism programmes with the engagement of the APA.
- Innovation in science and technology.
- Review all learning, development, and leadership strategies, products and services to ensure they meet the needs of policing and represent best value in terms of quality and cost. This includes developing an approach to leadership for ACPO with the support of the police service.
- Review recruitment and promotion activity to ensure that the best people are recruited and promoted. This includes developing succession planning to ensure that there is an adequate supply of talent at all levels.

In particular, the NPIA hope to improve the ability of the police service to manage and share effectively information across force boundaries. This it hopes to achieve through the IMPACT programme.

IMPACT

Managing police information effectively, and making it available wherever it is needed is crucial to police work. Forces in England and Wales operate more than 270 separate local databases and most of these do not communicate with each other, so information is not visible to other forces.

The IMPACT programme allows the police service to share information across boundaries, improving effectiveness. It was established as a result of the Bichard inquiry into the Soham murders, providing an IT solution to the sharing and management of information.

IMPACT Police National Database (PND)

The culmination of the IMPACT programme will be the implementation of the Police National Database (PND) in the year 2010. It will provide a powerful 'one-stop shop' for searching across forces' main operational information systems.

IMPACT Nominal Index

The IMPACT Nominal Index (INI) allows users to obtain information to make informed decisions, particularly those relating to protecting vulnerable children and spending less time searching for information and more time analysing and using it. Although initially deployed in child abuse investigation units, the system has been piloted in other areas and is now being rolled out to Scottish forces, the Police Service of Northern Ireland, and the British Transport Police.

The Code of Practice on the Management of Police Information

The Code of Practice on the Management of Police Information (MoPI) (Management of Police Information) is about making information relevant and accessible and ensuring that all police operational information is recorded, reviewed, shared, and deleted on a consistent basis across the police service.

The Code and its related guidance provide the information needed to make sure this happens. The MoPI team provides forces with practical advice and assistance in working towards compliance and is underpinned with a national training strategy.

The Police Leadership Quality Framework

The Police Leadership Quality Framework (PLQF) has been devised by NPIA on behalf of the Workforce Modernisation Board. It has been designed as a tool to help police leaders begin, or continue, to become an effective leader. The PLQF sets out to define leadership in terms of styles, values, ethics, standards, and competencies and lays out what each leader should aspire to become in pursuit of making British policing the best in the world.

The PLQF is the police service's statement on leadership based on the views of those who have first-hand knowledge of policing and also supports workforce modernization by providing a framework for a modern diverse workforce. It is an extension of the Integrated Competency Framework (ICF), and a leadership development tool that offers a means to improve the quality of police leaders.

Its emphasis on leadership qualities and values gives clarity and vision about what type of leadership the service wants. Used in conjunction with personal development plans it is a basis for recruitment, selection, and promotion, and assists in identification of 'exemplar' leadership.

The PLQF has identified three new 'core' leadership qualities:

- Personal integrity
- Personal awareness
- Passion for achievement.

It is these qualities that leaders within the police should aspire towards, and they also underpin the philosophy of this book, along with the requirement for extensive knowledge of how various groups within the service interact. The following considers the main staff and other associations that the police leader should have some knowledge about.

2.6 Staff Associations

The history of police staff associations can be traced back to the 19th century when officers were denied any rights of association, were poorly paid, worked long hours without days off and were subject to very strict discipline. Police strikes and the use of the military to restore and maintain order were not uncommon. The present prohibition on joining a trade union or taking strike action can be traced back to this early turbulent history. This section will now consider the various staff associations currently operating in the police service today.

2.6.1 The Police Superintendents' Association of England and Wales

The Police Superintendents' Association of England and Wales represents the interests of more than 1,600 Superintendents and Chief Superintendents. Association members work in all of the 43 Home Office police forces across England and Wales, the British Transport Police, and the Civil Nuclear Constabulary.

Whilst the 1919 Police Act created a Police Federation in England and Wales to represent officers below the rank of Superintendent, no formal provision was made for Superintendents. However, in 1920 the first central conference was arranged for Superintendents and this was the embryo for the present Superintendents' Association.

In 1952, following the Oaksey Committee Report, which had been set up to make recommendations on a number of matters impacting on police pay and conditions of service, the Police Superintendents' Association of England and Wales was formed. The Association survived and continued through the Willink Commission (1960), the Edmund-Davies Inquiry (1977), and the Sheehy Inquiry (1992) and remains the sole representative and negotiating body for Superintendents.

The broad objectives of the Superintendents' Association are as follows:

- To lead and develop the police service to improve the quality of our service delivery to local communities.

- To influence practice, policy, and decision-making at Chief Officer and government level.
- To provide appropriate support and advice to members regarding conditions of service.

2.6.2 The Police Federation

A brief history

The Police Federation of England and Wales is the representative body to which all police officers up to and including the rank of Chief Inspector belong. It was established by the Police Act in 1919, following a strike in London, when almost every constable and sergeant in the Metropolitan Police refused to go on duty. Officers were demanding a large pay increase, a widows' pension, the recognition of their then illegal trade union, and the reinstatement of those who had been dismissed for their union activities.

The Prime Minister of the time, David Lloyd George, gave in to the strikers on pay, but within months the 'Police Union' was removed and the Police Federation of England and Wales was established. Since that time, police officers have been prohibited from striking by statute, the most recent being the Police Act 1996. The Federation is not a union, but has a statutory responsibility to represent its members, that is all officers below the rank of Superintendent, in all matters affecting their welfare and efficiency.

The Federation today

The Federation today represents the interests of around 140,000 police officers, bringing together their views on welfare and efficiency to the notice of the government and all opinion formers. The Federation negotiates on all aspects of pay, allowances, hours of duty, annual leave, and pensions. It is consulted when police regulations are made, dealing with training, promotion, and discipline.

It takes an active interest in a wide range of subjects, which affect the police service, and puts forward its views on the members' behalf. Thus, it not only acts as a staff association, but also as a professional body, able to influence not only living standards, through pay and other benefits, but also the development of professional standards.

The Joint Branch Board

There are 43 police forces in England and Wales and each force has a Joint Branch Board (JBB.) The JBB in each force represents three constituent parts, elected by the Constables, Sergeants, and Inspectors (including Chief Inspectors). These are known as the Constables', Sergeants' and Inspectors' Branch Boards. They meet regularly to consider subjects affecting their ranks. However, much of their work is done together, when they meet as the JBB. They act as negotiating and consultative bodies in dealings with the Chief Constable, senior officers and the Police Authority, in matters affecting their force.

This structure provides an effective link between the officer, their force, and their representative Committee, in order to deal with day-to-day problems, and to improve the status of the police service and its members.

The Central Committees

Every three years, the Branch Board members elect a Central Committee for each rank, consisting of ten members. England and Wales is divided into eight regions and the 10 members of each separate Central Committee are elected as follows:

- One from each region except the Metropolitan region where two members are elected.
- One female reserve member.

These separate Central Committees elect their own officers and deal with national matters as they affect the rank they represent.

The Joint Central Committee

The Joint Central Committee (JCC) consists of representatives from each of the Constables', Sergeants' and Inspectors' Central Committees and is based at the Federation Headquarters in Surbiton. The JCC deals with all business affecting its members and is the policy-making body of the Federation. The JCC elects its national officers—the General Secretary, Chairman and Treasurer, and their Deputies. An Executive Committee, and a number of sub-committees covering specialist areas of interest, are made up from members of the JCC.

2.6.3 **UNISON**

UNISON is the biggest union in the police service, with over 30,000 police staff members in forces in England, Scotland, and Wales, and in NCS and NCIS. Every year, UNISON's trained representatives help thousands of police staff, providing expert protection and advice in the following areas:

- Disciplinary action
- Grievances
- IPCC investigations
- Professional standards enquiries.

It is police staff who underpin much police activity. UNISON's 35,000 members work in everything from administration and front desk roles to forensics and photography. Its members work in every police force in the UK, except Northern Ireland and the Metropolitan police which have different arrangements.

Members elect workplace stewards and safety reps and vote for branch officers. Every branch is supported by its nearest UNISON regional centre, where staff work with elected lay members. Each UNISON branch elects its own representatives to attend the UNISON National Delegate Conference and vote on behalf of all local branch members. Individuals are also elected through an annual individual ballot to UNISON's Police Staff National Service Group. This body helps decide policies and activities and works with UNISON staff to support members.

The union is represented on the Police Support Staff Council (PSSC) of England and Wales. The PSSC sets national terms and conditions for police support staff whilst in Scotland UNISON police members are covered by the PSSC Scotland.

The following staff groups also meet together under the UNISON umbrella:

- National Crime Squad members/National Criminal Intelligence Service members.
- Forensic Group of UNISON members.
- Police Community Support Officer working group.

2.7 Other Staff Associations

2.7.1 The National Black Police Association

The objective of the National Black Police Association (NBPA) is to promote good race relations and equality of opportunity within the police services of the UK and the wider community.

The NBPA works to place the Association at the heart of the police agenda. This is achieved by taking forward initiatives for the progression of minority officers and staff such as mentoring schemes, natural born leadership programme, and women in policing projects. The NBPA has a high profile within the Home Office and Government Strategic Committees and holds bi-lateral monthly meetings with the Minister. As well as sitting on a range of decision-making steering groups, the NBPA have regular meetings with the Heads of HMIC, ACPO, the Police Federation, UNISON, and BAWP amongst others. The Performance of the NBPA is recorded and documented to provide the widest sharing of information and learning and all the work of the Cabinet members and administrative team are governed by set policies and procedures to ensure transparency and accountability.

NBPA's mission

NBPA seeks to improve the working environment of black staff by protecting the rights of those employed within the police service and to enhance racial harmony and the quality of service to the black community of the UK. This assists the police service in delivering a fair and equitable service to all sections of the community.

Aims and objectives of the NBPA

The aims of the NBPA are to seek to improve the working environment of black staff members, as defined in article 4.1 of the constitution, employed within the police service of the UK, with a view to enhancing the quality of service to the minority ethnic community of the UK.

It does this by;

- Representing the views of all representative members of the Constituted Black Police Association (herein known as BPAs) who are affiliated to the NBPA.
- Providing a support network .
- Influencing the direction of policies nationally in line with equality issues and anti-discrimination policies in the police service and Wider Criminal Justice Systems.
- Advising and consulting on matters of racism, nationally.
- Working towards improving the relationship between the police and the minority community of the UK.
- Working towards improving the recruitment, retention, and progression of staff members within the police service.
- Assisting the police service in the development of new and existing policies, where necessary.
- Establishing relationships and working with other groups and individuals whose aims are compatible with or supportive of the NBPA.
- In pursuance of the above paragraph, the NBPA may exercise the following powers for the furtherance of its aims: To hold support meetings for members and other organizations.

From its inception it has sought to highlight issues faced by black staff in the police service, helping those in need of support by lending a listening ear and giving advice. The BPA continues to grow nationally along with similar organizations within other public sector organizations.

2.7.2 British Association for Women in Policing

The British Association for Women in Policing (BAWP) is partly a self-funded association although they now have the benefit of some funding from the Home Office, and are run on a voluntary basis by an Executive Committee consisting of serving and former police officers from across the UK.

The BAWP was formed in 1987 in order to fill a gap within the police service, with its main objectives to enhance the role and understanding of the specific needs of the women who are employed therein. Nationally, the BAWP is an associate member of the Women's National Commission and has links with the Equal Opportunities Commission. The BAWP is frequently asked to comment on topical issues and has contributed to a wide range of publications including national newspapers and magazines as well as police literature.

Internationally, the BAWP is affiliated to the International Association of Women Police, which is represented at the United Nations.

The BAWP has also established good working relationships with HMIC, Police Federation of England and Wales, Police Superintendents' Association, National Black Police Association, and Gay Police Association, in order to work together on issues of mutual concern.

The aims of BAWP are:

- To raise the awareness and understanding of issues affecting women within the police service.
- To facilitate and contribute to discussions on issues of concern to all officers—providing wherever possible the female perspective.
- To develop a network of professional and social contacts between officers nationally and internationally.
- To facilitate the sharing of information on issues affecting the service, and women in particular.
- To contribute to the continuous professional development of all members.

Many of the staff agencies and official bodies discussed within this chapter work together on a variety of policy groups and act as advisers to official bodies. Their aim is to ensure that the police organization provide the public with an efficient, effective, and economical service. Much of this approach is encapsulated in the title of 'performance management'.

2.8 Performance Management

The police service is a public body and depends on public money to carry out its functions. Therefore the public have a right to know how this money is being spent and how resources are being allocated to tackle crime and disorder in order to reassure the public. Police leaders should have some knowledge of these areas as they are often required to provide quality information in order for performance to be assessed.

2.8.1 Managerialism

Managerialism is the implementation of a variety of techniques generally copied from the private sector within a culture of cost efficiency and service effectiveness. This idea has been a point of reference for the police service for a number of years and manifests itself within the current climate of objectives, best value, and performance indicators. Consequently there are now several major bodies involved in examining the performance of the police service and the police practitioner should at least have a basic understanding of what they try to achieve. Some of these are illustrated below.

2.8.2 **How the police service is examined**

The Home Secretary introduces targets and ministerial priorities for the police service in England and Wales. These objectives are now encapsulated within the National Policing Plan 2005 to 2008 (Home Office 2004) and are summarized in the Key Point box below:

KEY POINT—FIVE KEY PRIORITIES FOR THE POLICE

The National Policing Plan 2005–2008 lists the five key priorities for the police service. These are as follows:

- to reduce overall crime-including violent and drug-related crime;
- to provide a citizen-focused police service which responds to the needs of the communities and the individuals inside those communities, especially witnesses and victims;
- to take action with partners to increase sanction detection rates and target prolific and other priority offenders;
- to reduce people's concerns about crime, anti-social behaviour, and disorder;
- to combat serious and organized crime, within and across force boundaries.

Further, the actions the police take to tackle crime and disorder are supported by the following:

- Local targets and objectives set for the force through the local policing plan published every year, the performance of which must be reported and published annually.
- Her Majesty's Inspectors of Constabulary (HMIC) and the Audit Commission also monitor, report, and publish figures on relative performance in dealing with specific matters as well as carrying out force inspections.
- The association of Chief Police Officers (ACPO) also report on public satisfaction under a variety of headings.
- There is a responsibility to report with the Crown Prosecution Service on Joint Performance Management including the submission of files of evidence.

2.8.3 **The Best Value Initiative**

The Local Government Act 1999 (Home Office 1999) introduced the Best Value Initiative which attempts to ensure the provision of better quality of services and value for money. This initiative applies to crime and disorder reduction partnerships and is achieved by reviews of the provision of services by local authorities (including police authorities) who are instructed to: 'Make arrangements to secure continuous improvements in the way in which they exercise their functions, having regard to a combination of economy, efficiency and effectiveness'.

Local authorities and the police are accountable to local people and are required to set standards for all services for which they are responsible. They are also required to undertake performance reviews of all their services over a five-year period to demonstrate that continuous improvements are being made.

The Government expects these reviews to:

- *Challenge* why, how, and by whom a service is being provided.
- Secure *comparison* with the performance of others.
- *Consult* local taxpayers, service users, etc. in the setting of new performance targets.
- Use fair and open *competition* wherever practicable as a means of securing efficient and effective services.

Consequently, there is a constant review of work being carried out in order to improve performance in line with the four Cs outlined above.

2.8.4 Best Value Performance Indicators

There are 94 Best Value Performance Indicators (BVPIs) described in the guidance document produced by the Office of the Deputy Prime Minister and are an integral part of local government's performance management framework. They constitute a framework of clear performance measures across the range of local government services and reflect the importance that is attached to service delivery at the local level. The BVPIs that apply to crime and disorder reduction revolve around burglary rates, violent crime, and racial offences along with others.

2.8.5 National and local priorities

However, national priorities alone cannot drive police activity—local priorities are a key concept for the police organization. Local political priorities are often determined by an area's problems. For example, if the police cover areas of high unemployment, poverty, social deprivation, or crime they may need to focus on tackling crime hotspots, providing support to vulnerable people, or helping to draw in investment to regenerate run-down areas as part of their role in Crime Reduction Partnerships. Alternatively, in a rural district council where crime is low but concern is disproportionately high, managing communications to dispel concern may be a high priority. Irrespective of local circumstances, the police need to engage and consult their local communities, gathering and sharing information that helps to determine their priorities.

A common public priority is reducing concern about crime. This is strongly affected by experience, deprivation levels and by the environmental quality of people's neighbourhoods. Similarly, rates of personal crime, such as robbery or assault, affect levels of neighbourhood concern about crime. Public priorities vary by region—where people live has a marked difference on levels of concern.

For example, there appears to be an interesting north-south divide between incidences of crime and concern about crime.

2.9 Summing Up

2.9.1 The tripartite system

This is the formal structure of police governance in England and Wales which was introduced by the Police Act 1964. It is commonly referred to as the tripartite system because accountability for policing lies between three distinct and separate bodies, namely the Chief Constable, local police authorities, and the Home Secretary, based in the Home Office.

2.9.2 ACPO

ACPO is an independent, professionally led strategic body in an equal and active partnership with Government and the Association of Police Authorities. ACPO leads and coordinates the direction and development of the police service in England, Wales, and Northern Ireland. In times of national need ACPO—on behalf of all chief officers—coordinates the strategic policing response.

2.9.3 The Association of Police Authorities

The Association of Police Authorities (APA) was set up on 1 April 1997 to represent police authorities in England, Wales, and Northern Ireland, both on the national stage and locally. It influences policy on policing and it supports local police authorities in their important role and, as such, the APA is the national voice of local police authorities.

The APA is funded by subscriptions from member authorities and has two main roles to perform. These are:

- to act as the national voice of all Police Authorities; and
- to help Police Authorities in doing their job locally.

2.9.4 Her Majesty's Inspectors of Constabulary

Her Majesty's Inspectors of Constabulary (HMIC) have been charged with examining and improving the efficiency of the police service in England and Wales (and latterly Northern Ireland), with the first HMIC appointed under the provisions of the County and Borough Police Act 1856. They are appointed by the Crown on the recommendation of the Home Secretary and report to Her Majesty's Chief Inspector of Constabulary (HMCIC), who is the Home Secretary's principal professional policing adviser. The HMCIC is independent both of the Home Office and of the police service.

2.9.5 The National Police Improvement Agency

The National Police Improvement Agency (NPIA) hopes to provide leadership and expertise to the service in areas as diverse as information and communications technology, support to information and intelligence sharing, core police processes, managing change and recruiting, developing and deploying people. As a single national organization the aim of the NPIA is to streamline and simplify the way policing improvement is delivered locally and nationally.

2.9.6 Staff associations

The history of police staff associations can be traced back to the 19th century when officers were denied any rights of association, were poorly paid, worked long hours without days off, and were subject to very strict discipline. Police strikes and the use of the military to restore and maintain order were not uncommon. The following are staff associations:

- The Superintendents Association of England and Wales
- The Police Federation
- UNISON
- The National Black Police Association
- The British Association for Women in Policing.

2.9.7 Performance management

The police service is a public body and depends on public money to carry out its functions. Therefore, the public have a right to know how this money is being spent and how resources are being allocated to tackle crime and disorder and also to reassure the public. Police leaders should have some knowledge of these areas as they are often required to provide quality information in order for performance to be assessed. Some of the performance management areas include:

- the National Policing Plan;
- the Best Value Initiative;
- National and local priorities.

References and Further Reading

Edmund Davies, Lord (1997) *Committee of Inquiry on the Police: Reports on negotiating machinery and pay*, London: HMSO.

Home Office (1964) *The Police Act*, London: Home Office,.

Home Office (1984) *The Police and Criminal Evidence Act*, London: Home Office,.

Home Office (1996) *The Police Act*, London: Home Office.

Newburn T. (ed.) (2005) *Policing-Key Readings*, Cullompton: Willan.

Newburn, T. and Reiner, R. (2007) *Policing and the Police*, in Maguire et al., *The Oxford Handbook of Criminology*, Oxford: Oxford University Press, 910–52.

Reiner, R. (2000) *The Politics of the Police*, Oxford: Oxford University Press.

Rogers, C. and Lewis, R. (2007) *Introduction to Police Work*, Cullompton: Willan.

Sheehy Inquiry (1992) *Report of Inquiry into Police Responsibilities and Rewards*, London: HMSO.

Willink, H.U. (1960) *Royal Commission on the Police*, London: HMSO.

Useful websites

The Association of Chief Police Officers available at <http://www.acpo.police.uk/>.
The Police Federation website available at <http://www.polfed.org/>.
The British Association of Women Police available at <http://www.bawp.org/index.php>.
The National Black Police Association available at <http://www.nbpa.co.uk/>.
The Gay Police Association available at <http://www.gay.police.uk/contact.html>.
UNISON union website available at <http://www.unison.org.uk/>.
The National Police Improvement Agency available at <http://www.npia.police.uk/>.
The Association of Police Authorities available at <http://www.apa.police.uk/apa>.
Her Majesties Inspectorate of Constabulary available at <http://inspectorates.home-office.gov.uk/hmic/>.
The Superintendents Association available at <http://www.policesupers.com/>.

SPACE FOR NOTES

SPACE FOR NOTES

SPACE FOR NOTES

SPACE FOR NOTES

3

Leading in Times
of Change

> Change is inevitable in a progressive country. Change is constant.
>
> (Benjamin Disraeli in a speech delivered in 1867)

3.1 **Introduction**

The police service has undergone an incredible amount of change in the past 10 to 15 years. This has manifested itself in many forms, but is mainly seen in the large number of Acts of Parliament such as the Crime and Disorder Act 1998 (Home Office 1998) which introduced the partnership approach to policing and the Police Reform Act 2002 (Home Office 2002) which introduced a number of dramatic changes in the way the police organize, plan, and deliver its services to the community. People often talk about the pace of change today. However, very few of us fully appreciate the effect of the very rapid changes that are taking place in the world around us. All change, however, will impact upon society.

Change is also necessary for modern day organizations to keep pace with changing society. We live in an increasingly diverse society with technology and public expectations being vastly different to just a few years ago. In order for the police to effectively deliver their services to this type of community, it must also be dynamic and understand that change is necessary if the police organization is to keep pace with society as a whole. For the police leader, therefore, understanding the dynamics of change, being able to manage change, and also to understand how to overcome resistance to change is a vital part of their job. An example of proposed change and the reaction to it is shown in scenario box below.

Scenario—The Sheehy Report

In the early 1990s, the Sheehy Report was published which looked at the core functions of the police in England and Wales. This was as a result of an in-depth study into the way the police service was run, including the rank structure and some of the main functions of the police. It raised many questions surrounding the efficiency and effectiveness of the police service and included many proposals which would have affected established working practices.

Consequently there was a major backlash organized by police officers including the police federation, and a national meeting was organized in London against the Report. This approach canvassed a lot of support from some politicians and a considerable amount of media attention was focused on the proposals. As a result, the majority of the suggestions were shelved and the amount of proposed change was minimized.

In practical terms, however, a change for the police organization means new legislation, new strategies and policies, and new structures to work within. Change cannot be imposed by the circulation of a memo or a document, or an e-mail. For change to work, all leaders in the police service must be prepared and willing to make sure that their colleagues make it work for them. Change management therefore requires the skills of leadership.

3.2 **Types of Change**

In general, change tends to manifest itself in one of two broad categories, namely gradual or radical change. However, within these occur a wide variety of types and combinations. Understanding the different types of change you are dealing with can help the leader to deal with change appropriately and to effectively interpret other people's attitude towards it. Both gradual and radical change can be proactive and reactive, according to whether the change is made voluntarily or in response to pressure from others. For the police service, for example, the introduction of centralized telephone call handling centres could be labelled a gradual reactive change in response to trying to find an efficient and economical way of dealing with an ever increasing number of calls, whilst a radical reactive change may the re-allocation of resources to a particular area following complaints from locally elected members regarding crime and disorder.

In the real world, however, change often combines both the reactive and the proactive elements within it.

3.2.1 **Gradual change**

This is a change that occurs slowly over a prolonged period at a more or less steady rate of intensity. It can involve just a few people, but is mostly seen as an unending organization-wide programme of change to improve quality of service and the processes behind the service delivery.

3.2.2 **Radical change**

This is a sudden dramatic change with marked effects. This change may occur as a result of unforeseen occurrences, such as a major disaster as seen in the recent cases of severe weather that caused flooding throughout England and Wales. It may involve a quick and radical change in methods that, until this point in time, may have served the organization well.

3.3 **External and Internal Forces for Change**

There are several major causes of change in society which directly affect policing. These are discussed in this section.

3.3.1 **Social causes**

General trends in society, politics, and demographics affect everyone. Recently these have resulted in large growth of youth and consumer markets, with what appears to be a shift from more community oriented life styles to a more individually centred society, coupled with an aging population in England and Wales. All organizations are affected by such changes and the police are no exception.

3.3.2 **Economic causes**

Economic changes are usually slow, but powerful. Even within what appears to be stable periods of broad economic stability, markets and monetary flows can move up or down sharply. Lack of money and resources has always appeared to be a perennial problem for the police service, and consequently government and other forms of economic changes greatly affect the way the police carry out their duties. Many forces have to be ready to adjust their spending plans by allowing for contingency funds for economic problems.

3.3.3 **Technological causes**

Perhaps this is the area that visibly manifests itself more than any other cause of change in society as a whole and within the police service in particular. The revolution in information technology is having an enormous impact upon methods of management, service delivery, and intelligence gathering within the police service. It is argued that this makes accomplishing tasks more efficient (for instance, the tasking of staff to appropriate jobs) and also to achieve new purposes (such as enhancing the ability to obtain better and more in-depth intelligence via covert means).

3.3.4 **Rising public expectations**

Today's public has been encouraged to expect more from their public services. They have also been encouraged to question far more why certain things are done in certain ways. For example, the many forms of the PACT (Partnerships And Community Talking) which underpins the idea of Neighbourhood Policing, is designed to encourage the community to tell the police want they want from them. The police service is part of the public sector, and as it is in central and local government, they are more accountable than ever before. The public also expect value for money and expect their police service to be a leaner and fitter organization.

3.3.5 **Service/force restructuring**

Over the past 10 to 15 years most large organizations in this country have restructured. The intention is that by making themselves leaner and fitter, and by cutting away any excess layers of management and waste, they will become more cost effective in the delivery of services to the public. There have been other innovations in the police service that affect police officers such as part-time working, family friendly policies, and the introduction of un-sworn personnel such as community support officers that are impact upon the force structure.

3.3.6 **New legislation**

Over the past 10 years the present government has introduced a large number of Acts of Parliament that directly affect the police service. For example, the Crime and Disorder Act 1998 (Home Office 1998) for the first time ensured by statute that the police engaged with other agencies to prevent and detect crime and disorder, whilst the Police Reform Act 2002 (Home Office 2002) is a major driver for change in the working practices and structure of the police in this country. Recent legislation to combat the rise in terrorism also affects the police organization, as does the introduction of the Serious Organised Crime Agency which was created under an Act of Parliament. However, we must remember that the police service is also affected by what other types of Acts of Parliament such as legislation regarding health and safety, human rights, and race relations. On top of this, we must never forget that Britain is part of the European Union and has to abide by laws made by that organization as well. All this means that in terms of legislation, the police service has been influenced, and probably will for the foreseeable future, and will undergo some change as a result of the introduction of new legislation.

Having discussed some of the drivers for change, stop a while and try to complete the following exercise.

EXERCISE 3A

1. Try to identify the impact of IT developments in the community where you live.
2. What changes have taken place in the population where you live?
3. What impact do you think an increasing public expectation has had on your local police?
4. How do you think force restructuring will affect the way your community is policed?

Once you reflect upon some of these issues, you can clearly see how change is all around us.

3.4 **Responses to Change**

Resistance to change should not be regarded as unnatural or just someone being obstructive. Change can cause great stress to people. Before moving on try Exercise 3B below and see how you reacted.

EXERCISE 3B

Think of a time when you have undergone a major change in your life. It could be the death of a relative, the birth of a child, or some other significant event. Reflect a while, and then write down how you believe you felt as a result of these changes.

You may have written down all or some of the following:

- Fear
- Anger
- Resistance
- Welcome
- Happiness
- Didn't care.

All of these are natural reactions to change.

People affected by change will vary in their response to it. Those people who are in charge of introducing and overseeing the implementation of change should be aware of how varied this response can be and also be equipped to deal with it. However, we need to understand that what is not known causes fear and induces resistance. Restructuring within an organization can leave people uncertain about their future prospects and even about their current job and people want to feel secure and have some control over the changes that are taking place. Further, not knowing the reasons for the change also causes resistance. It is very often unclear to those involved why the change is necessary at all and change can result in a loss of power and/or a loss of benefits for people.

Try to recall a time in your working life when a process of change was going on around you. This could be a new policy, a change in the organization, or even a change in your working procedures. Consider the following questions;

- Where you consulted or were the changes imposed?
- Why do you think this was?
- Were your feelings the same as your work colleagues?

By answering the above questions and attempting the exercises in this chapter so far, we have started a process whereby we can start to analyse the issues driving change, the outcomes of the change, and how people feel about it. A leader is a vital part of managing this change process. However, if a leader is to successfully implement change, they need to have an understanding of how change may be received.

3.5 **Some Reasons why Colleagues are Concerned with Change**

Whilst there are likely to be many reasons why colleagues will be concerned by change there are several main areas that can be identified. These are discussed below.

3.5.1 **The so-called comfort zone**

People who want to provide an efficient and effective police service to the public believe they can only achieve this by working in an environment where they are relatively happy. They regard this environment as one where they are familiar with the ways things are done, and where they believe they know and trust the colleagues they work with. This is our so-called 'comfort zone'.

For example, structural change involving the creation of working neighbourhood policing teams could mean that suddenly people are working with not only people they may consider to be strangers, but also with people who are not the same as them in terms of job specification and working arrangements, such as police officers and community support officers. People may even be fearful that their jobs may become too difficult or even will disappear altogether.

Legislation can revolutionize the way the police carry out their role. The Crime and Disorder Act 1998 introduced multi-agency working which meant that a new way of thinking about delivery of police services with partners was required.

Both of these examples mean that people may find themselves working in an environment where they are not sure how to do things and therefore this may lead to less efficiency.

3.5.2 **Previous experiences**

Such is the rate of change experienced by public bodies such as the police that many people employed by the organization have been through the change process before.

How they were supervised and managed through that period of change will have a major influence on how their receptiveness to new ideas during a new period of change. If these previous experiences left them with a feeling that change is just a 'top-down' process that is dictated to them, especially if they felt that they lost more than they gained, then they are bound to be wary of new ideas. Not many people would openly welcome change if it meant this type of implementation and as such most people would not only fear change, but would openly avoid it. Even if it cannot be avoided, then it may lead to the change being sabotaged.

3.5.3 **Impact upon personal lives**

This area may not be considered too much by those planners who impose change within the police service. However, it is as vital an area as any other when it comes to trying to understand resistance to change. However, it is a fact that we all plan our lives on what we know. For example, we make arrangements for summer holidays based on our earnings and working arrangements. Most of us make decisions about our life in a similar fashion. We are comfortable presuming it will be the same next year as it is now. Change can threaten this and our future plans are not so easy to plan anymore.

This brief outline explains why many people fear change. Supervisors need to be aware of these issues (and other that may surface) and take them into account when they are managing the change process.

3.6 Dealing with the Implementation of Change

Now that we have considered some reasons why change occurs in organizations and how that change affects or can be resisted by some people, we need to consider how best to implement change.

EXERCISE 3C

Think of two examples of change, one where the change was managed more or less effectively and one where it was not so well managed.

Effective   *Not so effective*

Compare your effective and the not-so-effective methods of introducing change. Do you detect some themes? You may have discovered that where change was effectively managed, the supervisors involved those who were directly affected in lots of different ways.

Whilst in general there are many ways in which we can manage change, there are two main areas that the police supervisor needs to consider which are also the most common when one considers the best methods of implementing change. These are:

- involve colleagues in the implementation process; and
- something called 'leverage'.

3.6.1 Involving colleagues

Earlier, we discussed how people see change as a real threat and this can cause fear and resistance. To remove this distrust completely is impossible, because of the effect of change on people's perceptions and their lives. However, poor leadership techniques can intensify and magnify the fear and apprehension people feel about change. One of the ways that this is likely to happen is if there is a lack of communication or dialogue with those who will be affected by change. Involving people in the change process encourages communication and dialogue. By involving people at an early stage in the change process, people will feel that they have some influence over events, both in the way change is introduced and also in the end result. This enables them to feel valued, and also injects the feeling of ownership tied into the intended outcomes and changes.

This involvement also provides the supervisor with some form of feedback on how the change is progressing as we can learn much by listening to those who are going through the change process. The reasons why we should involve colleagues is summarized in the following Key Point box.

KEY POINT—REASONS FOR INVOLVING COLLEAGUES IN THE CHANGE PROCESS

1. It promotes communication and dialogue.
2. Involvement will reduce the likelihood of fear of change.
3. Colleagues can influence the process and it engenders ownership of the outcomes.
4. Involvement provides feedback for the supervisor.

3.6.2 Leverage

There is a major benefit in involving colleagues in the change process. Involvement of people can provide something called 'leverage'. This is a key element in most strategies for introducing change. Leverage is the creation of a lever providing strategic advantage.

Wherever we work we are part of a system. Each of us depends upon others within the system as others are dependent upon us to perform our jobs. For example, a police officer who attends at the scene of a house burglary as a first response should ensure the scene is preserved in order that the scenes of crime officer who attends will have every chance of obtaining evidence. The chain is a workplace *system*. When you have thought about this for a moment, try and complete Exercise 3D below.

EXERCISE 3D

Imagine you are a sergeant and try to identify some of the systems or parts of systems you are responsible for. Write down what you think these may be.

You may have included in the exercise above something like the following:

- overtime for your staff;
- submission of files of evidence;
- attending public meetings.

You may have thought of many others but the point is that the process of change not only impacts upon individuals in the workplace but also upon the systems as well. The clever supervisor is the person who identifies the point in the system where there will be the greatest leverage, and this is usually where it will be easiest to generate the greatest commitment to change. This is done by identifying the position in the system where there is the greatest disadvantage or weakness. Where there is a flaw in the system, the supervisor will generally tend to find a willingness to overcome it.

Therefore, supervisors must, at the beginning of the change process, try to obtain leverage. They must identify the place where the commitment of individuals will be the greatest. The greater the commitment to change the greater the momentum will be created. The more everyone is then committed to the need for change the greater the 'lever'. There can be no change without a lever, and if people are turned off by the idea, then there will be an unsuccessful change process.

3.7 Organizational Culture and Change

Bringing about change and overcoming resistance to it can be managed both wisely and humanely. By first understanding organizational culture, which is much like an organization having a personality, we can delve deeper into the key aspects of organizational change.

3.7.1 **Organizational culture**

Many forces shape an organizations culture. Often its origins lie in its values, administrative procedures, and the personalities of those people at the top of the organization who have a vision of how things should be done. For example, an individual Chief Constable will sometimes influence the culture of their particular police force by their vision of community and race relations, or roads policing.

Organizational culture therefore responds to and reflects the conscious and unconscious choices, behaviour patterns, and prejudices of top-level managers. As they leave or become less active, other top-level managers help redefine the organizational culture.

The culture in which a society operates also helps determine the culture of the organization. Sooner or later, society's norms, beliefs, and values find their way into the organization. For example, if society becomes more tolerant with regards to the use of cannabis, politicians may alter existing legislation to amend the criminal use of such a drug. This in turn will affect the working practices of the police and impact upon the organizational culture that has a view about drug users in general.

The specific area in which an organization works also helps shape its culture. For example, the culture of the police service is quite different from a high tech information technology firm specializing in computer software. Another area where an organization can be influenced is through its code of conduct. The code of conduct should establish the workplace culture and communicates the employer's true attitudes to its workforce. We have witnessed in recent times the change within the police service from the use of a 'Discipline Code' which laid emphasis upon discipline through the rank system to the implementation of a 'Code of Conduct' which allows for a less threatening system, with checks and balances for due process.

3.7.2 **Elements of organizational culture**

The elements of a culture can help to explain the nature of the subtle forces that influence the actions of staff. For example, a workplace culture that values high risk taking and cutting corners can often lead to trouble when procedures are not followed correctly. For example, not following procedures correctly when interviewing a suspect on the belief that they will plead guilty is a risky thing to do. If that person seeks legal advice, not only could the officer lose the case, but may find him/herself having to explain their actions to others.

There are several influential elements of an organizational culture. These are:

- *Values.* Values are the foundation of any organization. The philosophy of an organization is expressed through its values and it is hoped these values guide behaviour on a daily basis. Research has shown that when supervisors and managers have a lax attitude towards honesty, employee theft increases to above 30 per cent (Kanter 1983). Most police forces now issue a statement outlining their values and commitments.

- *Myths.* The police service is an occupation that has more than its fair share of stories and myths. Simon Holdaway (Holdaway 1983), in his seminal study of the police service refers to these myths as 'folk stories'. They are dramatic narratives or imagined events about the history of the organization or people within the organization that help unify groups but also provide negative stereotypes about sections of the community.
- *Rites and rituals.* An organization's culture is highly influenced by some of its rights and rituals as it can reinforce the informal hierarchy that exists between groups of people in their workplace. Few organizations, including the police, would admit they have them, but the idea that the latest probationer on the shift makes the tea for everybody else is just one such ritual.

In addition to the dominant culture in an organization, there are usually found subcultures that also influence behaviour. A subculture is a small pocket of activity that differs from the main culture of the organization. For example, working practices within a small independent, plain clothes unit dealing with drugs enforcement will have a different culture from a uniform response unit as they have more time to engage in 'slow-time' police work involving intelligence gathering whilst the response unit has to deal with 'quick-time' decision-making.

3.7.3 How people learn the culture

People learn the organizational culture primarily through socialization which is the process of coming to understand the values, norms, and customs for adapting to the organization. Socialization is therefore a method of indoctrinating employees into the organization in such a way that they perpetuate the culture. The socialiaation process takes place mostly by learning through intimidation and observation.

Another way in which people learn the culture is through the teachings of leaders and supervisors. This is an important point to remember for leaders, as a good role model can influence a person's performance as a police employee for over 30 years of their working life.

KEY POINT—THE LEADER AS ROLE MODEL

A leader should be a good role model as they have the power to influence others in the way they carry out their job for the rest of their career.

3.8 **An Example of Change—the National Workforce Modernisation Programme**

3.8.1 **Background**

In October 2005, ACPO council approved a draft ACPO vision for workforce modernization. Since that time this has been expanded upon to highlight the business case and benefits for the police service by introducing these modernization ideas and change. It is acknowledged that the job of policing is getting bigger, wider, and deeper, with criminality on one hand getting more sophisticated and complex, requiring equally sophisticated policing methods, delivered within a tight regulatory framework and in an ethical manner; and on the other hand the service is still expected to provide a capability to deal with the enormous volume of routine police work and reassuring visibility for a society which demands high quality and more bespoke service. With the drive to control anti-social behaviour and the emergence of radical terrorism, there is a need to be able to mass produce and deliver community intelligence, low level enforcement, visible patrol, and public contact at unprecedented levels. The workforce modernization scheme, however, intends to retain core operational competencies in order to maintain flexibility of deployment.

3.8.2 **The constable**

Even with the introduction of community support officers and other changes in personnel, it is virtually impossible to think of a British police service that does not contain an attested office holder, nor a service that has the role of constable reduced to such an extent that it is unable to fulfil its fundamental obligations. That said, the police service needs to 'up-skill' staff to undertake the critical tasks which involve:

- the use of coercive power;
- providing the highest quality of evidence in court; and
- undertaking complex operational activities.

Omni-competence or 'jack of all trades' approach can no longer support the way in which the police service undertakes its duties. The rise in the number of specialist squads and departments is testament to new and growing demands on the police which will mean change within the organization. The office of constable is central to these changes however. Embodied within the role of the constable are three crucial elements that the police service needs to retain. These are:

- Flexibility—to provide resilience and sustainable responses to all types of emergencies.
- Independence—of the holder of the office of constable to act with individual discretion and in an ethical manner.
- Public confidence—a crucial element which underpins the service, through public acceptance.

Because of these main elements the office of constable needs to be retained within any future changes in the workforce.

3.8.3 **Future workforce**

The workforce for the police service being proposed is one of an operational workforce which has a greater mix, where police staff, with and without designated powers, support warranted police officers in a seamless and functional fashion. This means that policing will move from the one-dimensional police officer/staff model to a wider team approach to policing applying the required and appropriate skills and powers to the job in hand. Consequently, any future structure of the police workforce will include the following:

- Much greater specialisms to better meet any tasks required to be undertaken and the skills and experience to carry them out.
- Different tiers of practitioners to provide a more flexible approach to tackling high volume and complex workloads.
- Seamless organizational model which is inclusive of police officer and other police staff.
- Better workforce planning particularly in terms of recruitment and training, which includes greater use of Higher and Further education facilities.

3.8.4 **Career pathways**

It is against this background that the idea of major change in the career structure of police officers is proposed, that of career pathways. This introduces the concept of a wider mix of staff, including non-warranted, designated, and warranted staff who have greater accredited and specialization of skills. Whilst maintaining the office of constable, the service will become more professional and can deliver increased performance, productivity, and impact. In order for this to be achieved, four core capabilities of policing are proposed, namely:

- Intelligence
- Investigation
- Neighbourhoods
- Response.

This framework will form the basis of the workforce structure, enabling more accurate succession planning and will allow individuals to undertake continuous professional development in a particular capability, moving away from omni-competence towards greater specialization of skills to meet present and future policing demands. Having read through the workforce modernization programme information, attempt the exercise in the following box.

EXERCISE 3E

Knowing the problems of introducing change within the workplace, write down some of the things that you think may occur due to the introduction of the workforce modernization programme. Discuss this with your friends or colleagues.

Once you have done this, consider how best to assist the introduction of the new scheme?

In conclusion, the police service is undergoing large changes in structure, working arrangements, and staff appointments. Having an understanding of how these changes come about, their impact and influence on individuals within the force, and how to manage these changes for people is a vital skill for police leaders.

3.9 Summing Up

3.9.1 Types of change

Gradual change

This is a change that occurs slowly over a prolonged period at a more or less steady rate of intensity. It can involve just a few people, but is mostly seen as an unending organization-wide programme of change to improve quality of service and the processes behind the service delivery.

Radical change

This is a sudden dramatic change with marked effects. This change may occur as a result of unforeseen occurrences, such as a major disaster as seen in the recent cases of severe weather that caused flooding throughout England and Wales. It may involve a quick and radical change in methods that, until this point in time, may have served the organization well.

3.9.2 Internal and external forces for change

Social causes

General trends in society, politics, and demographics affect everyone.

Economic causes

Economic changes are usually slow, but powerful. Even within what appears to be stable periods of broad economic stability, markets and monetary flows can move up or down sharply.

Technological causes

The revolution in Information Technology is having an enormous impact upon methods of management, service delivery, and intelligence gathering within the police service.

Rising public expectations

Today's public has been encouraged to expect more from their public services. They have also been encouraged to question far more why certain things are done in certain ways.

Service/force restructuring

Over the past 10 to 15 years most large organizations in this country have restructured. The intention is that by making themselves leaner and fitter, and by cutting away any excess layers of management and waste, they will become more cost effective in the delivery of services to the public.

New legislation

Over the past 10 years the present government has introduced a large number of Acts of Parliament that directly affect the police service. For example, the Crime and Disorder Act 1998 for the first time ensured by statute that the police engaged with other agencies to prevent and detect crime and disorder.

3.9.3 Responses to change

Resistance to change should not be regarded as unnatural or just someone being obstructive. Change can cause great stress to people. It can include all or some of the following:

- Fear
- Anger
- Resistance
- Welcome
- Happiness
- Didn't care.

3.9.4 Best methods of dealing with change

Whilst in general there are many ways in which we can manage change, there are two main areas that the police supervisor needs to consider which are the most common when one considers the best methods of implementing change. These are:

- Involve colleagues in the implementation process; and
- Something called 'Leverage'.

3.9.5 **The National Workforce Modernisation Programme**

This programme is the background to the introduction of much change in the structure and the workforce of the police organization in England and Wales. In order for this to be achieved, four core capabilities of policing are proposed, namely:

* Intelligence
* Investigation
* Neighbourhoods
* Response.

This framework will form the basis of the workforce structure, enabling more accurate succession planning and will allow individuals to undertake continuous professional development in a particular capability, moving away from omni-competence towards greater specialization of skills to meet present and future policing demands.

References and Further Reading

Holdaway, S. (1983) *Inside the British Police—A Force at Work*, Oxford: Blackwells.
Home Office (1998) *The Crime and Disorder Act*, London: HMSO.
Home Office (2002) *The Police Reform Act*, London: HMSO.
Kamp, J. and Brooks, P. (1991) *Perceived Organizational Climate and Employee Counter-Productivity*, Journal of Business and Psychology, Summer, 1991, 455.
Kanter, R.M. (1983) *The Change Masters*, New York: Simon & Schuster.
The Oxford Dictionary of Thematic Quotations (2000) Oxford: Oxford University Press.

Useful websites

Police Leadership Quality Framework available at <http://www.npia.police.uk/en/6940.htm>.
The Association of Chief Police Officers available at <http://www.acpo.police.uk/>.
The National Police Improvement Agency available at <http://www.npia.police.uk/>.
The Serious Organised Crime Agency available at <http://www.soca.gov.uk/>.

SPACE FOR NOTES

SPACE FOR NOTES

SPACE FOR NOTES

Supporting Leadership

4

Leading From the Front

4.1 **Introduction**

In general, leadership is regarded as key to performance, and within the police service is a fundamental area within the police reform agenda. Research conducted by the Home Office (Home Office 2004) identified that people who work in the police organization want their leaders to acknowledge their contribution. The research also suggests that there are four areas that can be linked to effective leadership. These are:

- Being committed to achieving a high quality service to the community and supporting staff to achieve this.
- Displaying high personal and professional standards and challenging poor behaviour.
- Enabling, valuing and developing staff.
- Having relevant knowledge and skills.

Whilst the research highlighted the positive attributes of good leaders, it also suggested a number of discernible behaviours seen in some leaders, namely being lazy, unethical, and not dealing with poor or unacceptable performance and behaviour. Unfortunately, many of these negative behaviours identified by the research tended to occur together in the same leaders, with many of the interviewees in the research describing at least one leader who displayed multiple negative behaviours. Consider what you want from a leader and attempt Exercise 4A below.

EXERCISE 4A   Characteristics of a leader

Think of people whom you consider as a good or bad leader. What is it about them that influenced your decision?

4.2 **The Ability to Lead**

Sometimes leaders forget to observe all the rules of good leadership because not everyone has the ability to remember everything! Many successful leaders use different ways to lead, and not all people are 'born' leaders. Many people adopt different methods to suit their own personality, proving perhaps that leadership is a skill to be learned. No one is the perfect supervisor or leader, but a person can become a better administrator if they remember three things. These are:

- Identify as many of your own shortcomings as possible and work to improve them. This requires an honest and reflective approach to thinking about yourself.
- Practice your leadership characteristics as much as possible. This could be patience, being decisive, being approachable etc.

- Time and effort are required but practice will improve your performance as a supervisor. As a leader you may have to sell yourself to others, and one way of doing this is to gain respect.

4.3 **Winning Respect**

A good leader will always have the respect of others, as it is easier for people to give their loyalty and have confidence in those they respect. Lack of respect for a leader is usually the precursor for lack of respect for instructions, advice, and other communications from the leader. There are several areas that the good leader can encourage amongst staff that will enhance respect for their leadership abilities. These are discussed below.

4.3.1 **Encourage staff to speak freely**

Too many leaders encourage their staff to just say 'yes' to anything they say as they are not able to take criticism or any objections to their ideas. In an historical and political sense leaders who have not encouraged their staff to speak openly and frankly, have suffered from bad decision-making. Irving Janis (1982) coined the term 'group-think' to explain the dangers of group conformity, where individuals who were afraid to speak their minds went along with a plan despite their grave misgivings. Janis cites the USA's foiled invasion of Cuba in what became known as the Bay of Pigs fiasco during the early 1960s as an example where people close to the US President believed the plan would fail, but had never been encouraged to disagree with him.

By failing to encourage free speech, the leader loses the benefit of independent ideas, information on operations that may require attention, correction, or improvement as well as the respect from others. Good leaders should welcome suggestions and criticism and reflect upon them, and if valid, take action to implement them. Never be afraid to seek out suggestions and ideas from others.

4.3.2 **Keep up to date**

Most people want a leader who knows what is going on in the workplace, and more importantly what is likely to come their way in terms of work expectations of the organization. A good leader therefore keeps him/herself up to date with what kind of job is being done by staff, what the job conditions are like, what changes are likely to occur that affect the way the job is being done, and how any changes in operating procedures may affect everyone.

If you as a leader show that you have a distinct lack of knowledge which underpins your statements, actions, and decisions this could diminish the respect people have for you as a leader. You must try to keep up to date and the following will help you in this function:

- Subscribe or otherwise obtain and read the regular police type journals that are now available throughout the country.
- Read the policy and advice documents published by your force on various matters and visit your own force website.
- Regularly visit the official websites of important websites of groups such as ACPO, HMIC, APA, the Home Office, and the Police Federation.
- Make sure you watch or listen to news broadcasts—invariably there is something on about the police, crime, and disorder.

Spending time with people whom you lead and asking them questions in casual conversation sometimes introduces you to something you were not aware of. However, always remember that you should never violate a confidence if it is shared with you by those you lead.

4.3.3 **Acknowledge good work with praise**

Praise stimulates good work and is a good motivator for staff. We all like to be liked, and giving praise is an important part of being a leader. A good point to remember is that praise should be given publicly as it has extra weight and raises moral, standing, and self-confidence in the person receiving it. Other people see that good work is acknowledged and that deserving people are not overlooked. Don't forget that public praise can be written or verbal, but whatever way you choose to do it make sure that it is known that praise is given. Praise need not be complex or difficult. A few honest words of admiration for a person's effort are often appreciated. For example, a few words in the parade room or office to a staff member about the professional way in which they dealt with an incident, or the manner in which a report was compiled or submitted is of great importance and helps to break down barriers.

4.3.4 **Be consistent**

Being consistent is necessary to maintain the momentum of an organization. Leaders who introduce changes without warning, issue abrupt or conflicting orders, or introduce other inconsistencies create confusion amongst staff. Your attempt at winning respect will deteriorate quickly as a result of inconsistency. Consistency in attitude and manner is also very important. A leader who is moody, for example being alternately cheerful then down in the mouth, is not a true leader. Neither is one who is friendly one day then unfriendly the day after. People will not respect you as a leader if you display these attributes, they will be cautious and bewildered, not knowing what to expect from you.

4.3.5 **Display high levels of personal integrity**

Whilst any leader must be proficient in his or her speciality and leadership techniques, this alone is not enough. Leaders must learn self-control and display a mature moral view as well as professional ethical and moral principles. A good leader must actually do what is expected of him or her, and also do what is expected of others. They must not engage for example in activities that may lead to the misuse of police equipment or supplies. The good leader must exhibit promptness, be dependable, and always be courteous to others. People who you are expected to lead will not respect you as a leader if your conduct and actions are not of the highest level, or if you advocate different standards for them than you apply to yourself.

4.3.6 **Be professional**

Being businesslike in your attitude conveys assurance to others that you take your responsibilities seriously. When you conduct yourself with dignity, it is still possible to be cheerful, pleasant, and friendly without engaging in horseplay, particularly at inappropriate times. Subordinates may be amused by a leader who engages in this type of activity, but will not respect or even accept leadership from that individual.

Try not to defer decisions. The clear inference by delay is that the leader lacks knowledge or sometimes courage. Making decisions promptly does not mean making them hastily: some delay may be necessary to obtain all the facts. Sometimes the leader may not know the answer to the question, but if immediate action is not taken to arrive at an answer, people will still respect the leader.

4.4 **Winning Confidence of Others**

An effective leader must have the confidence of those that he or she leads. Most people will not be loyal to a supervisor if they do not trust them. A lack of confidence in a leader can introduce a lack of confidence in instructions and action plans so the issues of loyalty, morale, respect, and personal attitude to work are vital if those who are led are confident in their leaders.

4.5 **The Importance of Loyalty**

Loyalty is essentially an emotional feeling rather than an intellectual commitment. It is not one sided and people who are led will only feel loyal to their leaders if the leader is loyal to them. Friendship sometimes plays a large part in encouraging loyalty, making it hard to imagine people being un-loyal to a friendly leader. However, one must remember the saying that 'familiarity breeds contempt' when dealing with people, and that a balance needs to be struck between being friendly and letting people treat you in such a manner. After all, there may be occasions when a leader needs people to act quickly and decisively, and when loyalty is necessary. Friendliness does not imply that a leader suffers from being weak or that he/she has no discipline. It shows that, as a leader, you have an interest in caring for the individuals that you lead. However, there may be a downside to loyalty that needs to be considered. If the leader is unethical in their performance and the people that they lead are loyal, then they too are likely to be unethical in their performance. This can lead not only to corruption, but inequality in the delivery of policing services.

There are several important ways in which loyalty can be obtained and maintained. These are:

- By being pleasant. Being pleasant invariably means that you are seen as being approachable. It produces an environment where people are not afraid to speak to you, and overcomes and smoothes obstacles in the workplace.
- Being available. A leader who is distant and difficult to talk to does not encourage good relationships with people. However, this must be balanced with the ability of the leader to complete their own workload.
- By being sympathetic and empathizing with others. This is the ability to see a problem from the viewpoint of the other person or to put oneself in the other person's shoes. People invariably have some sort of problem, either work or home related. Leaders must try to understand that people with problems sometimes cannot effectively fulfil their role, so this person must be important to the leader.
- Realizing that team members are people. An organization is made of people and they should be respected as valued individuals. People have aspirations, hopes and plans, training, experience, likes and dislikes, as well as preferences and deficiencies. It is possible to direct people to complete a task, but to do so without realizing that you are dealing with people is not leadership.
- Show concern for health and safety issues at work. Whilst this is catered for largely by legislation, as a leader you should always be aware of the safety implications for staff in whatever situation you find yourself in. Such concern gives a good leader an opportunity to develop loyalty.
- Be impartial. Good leaders should not form decisions on the basis of prejudice or on the basis of insufficient information. Further, favouritism, which is the giving of a greater number of privileges to an individual than that person deserves, should never be part of a leader's decision-making process.

4.6 **The Role of Morale**

The morale of people in the workplace should be one of the most important considerations of any leader. Morale is not something that is easily identified, but simply means the zeal, enthusiasm, or belief which underpins a person's or group's work or task. Morale within the police service is doubly important as it can not only have an impact within the organization, but can also affect he service provided to the general public as well. A good leader must understand what moral is and recognize its importance. Further, the leader needs to know how to maintain good morale amongst the people he/she works with.

4.6.1 **The importance of morale**

Merely possessing the skills necessary to be a good employee of the police organization, coupled with the necessary equipment, are not enough to produce a person who performs to their highest ability. In order to appreciate this, try Exercise 4B below.

EXERCISE 4B Morale

Think about people who you work with or know. Try to identify someone whom you think has something called high morale. What is it about them that makes you think they have this? Write a list of the things that you can think of.

The components of moral, that of being enthusiastic, willing to work as part of a team, and an inclination to get personal satisfaction from doing a job well are very important to achieving success. The reason why this is so important is that, as a leader, you need people who have high moral because high moral amongst individuals is linked to high productivity and quality of work produced by the individual and the team.

People with high morale approach their jobs and dealing with members of the public in a more positive light, and this encourages fewer problems. These individuals tend to remain within the police service longer, and everyone benefits from their experience and training invested in them over the years.

Motivating individuals and maintaining morale is dealt with in more depth in Chapter 8.

4.7 **Developing Individuals**

Leaders and supervisors need to understand that part of leading from the front is their role in developing those individuals whom they work with or are part of their team. Developing individuals does not always mean formal training courses for people although these are vital. Sometimes on-the-job training is an effective way of developing people, and this can be done in the main by coaching or mentoring.

4.7.1 **Leaders as coaches**

Coaching has been defined as helping and supporting people to manage their own learning in order to maximize their potential, develop their skills, and improve their performance (Parsloe 2004).

KEY POINT—COACHING DEFINED

Coaching is helping and supporting people to manage their own learning and maximizing their potential to develop their skills and improve their performance.

Coaching, therefore, is helping people in the workplace to expand and grow and this in turn will improve them as individuals and their workplace performance.

The more inexperienced a staff member is then the leader should engage in a more practical coaching style. The style that coaches usually adopt is sometimes called the experiential learning cycle. This occurs where an activity is demonstrated to an individual then the coach and staff member reflect upon what has happened. The next stage is where people try to make sense of what has happened, whilst the final stage involves putting what has been learnt into practice. This approach is sometimes referred to as the experiential cycle of learning. The cycle can be seen in Figure 4.1 below.

Figure 4.1 The experiential learning cycle

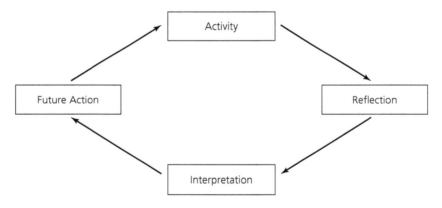

By continually applying this approach to dealing with workplace issues, problems, and activities, the staff member will not only learn how to complete tasks, but also start to become a reflective practitioner, and more professional in their role.

4.7.2 **Leaders as mentors**

Mentoring includes coaching, facilitating, counselling, and networking. The mentor not only shows an individual how to do a job, but also provides encouragement and shares enthusiasm for the job in hand. Whilst coaching is an enabling and helping process, mentoring is more of a supportive role. Therefore not everyone may have the qualities required of a mentor. Before moving on, consider Exercise 4C below.

EXERCISE 4C Qualities of a mentor

Reflect upon the people you work with, and consider one whom you may think of as being suitable as a mentor. What qualities do you think they possess?

You may have thought of some of the following which are considered as essential for the mentoring role. The person must:

- be a good motivator;
- be a high performer;
- be responsible;
- possess good interpersonal skills;
- be a good teacher;
- possess a high level of workplace knowledge.

Clearly, these individuals are an important asset to the police leader in helping produce individuals who are professional and competent at their jobs.

4.8 Time Keeping and Time Management

As a leader, people look to you for example. Therefore the efficient use of your time is critical. Much of a leader's time is spent reacting to other individuals or incidents so it is important that as a leader you have some form of strategy for dealing with the routine events such as delegation and for identifying priorities. Leaders need:

- time to think;
- time for people; and
- time to grow as individuals.

Therefore, a skilled leader should be able to manage their own time. If you cannot organize yourself, how can you organize anyone or anything else? Time keeping and time management are important for any leader.

Time management is made up of applying some underlying principles. Knowing your purpose, aims, and objectives are important. Part of the success in managing your time lies in building a clearly defined picture of your role. Writing a role requirement allows you to remove those tasks which can be discarded; you can then clearly focus on your true role. One of the reasons why leaders don't have enough time is because they are often engaged in traditional but unnecessary tasks. By defining your own role you may be able to save quite a lot of time.

However, even when you consider your basic tasks, you may feel that you are still short of time. Exercise 4D below will help you understand some ways in which you may improve your use and allocation of time.

EXERCISE 4D

Read the list below and place a cross in the boxes opposite the methods you would like to improve on.

Don't engage in gossip		Plan routine tasks for the day	
Plan phone conversations beforehand		Be punctual for appointments	
Plan meetings effectively beforehand		Store information so it is readily accessible	
Make decisions without undue delay		Don't try to solve everyone's problems	
Phone or e-mail rather than travel to meet someone		Deal with people who interrupt you in the correct manner	
Delegate correctly to staff			

4.9 Time Management and Paperwork

If you ask people for the worst thing about working in the police service, invariably they will point out the enormous amount of paperwork involved in the bureaucracy that supports the police as an organization. Indeed, the recent report on the police service published by Sir Ronnie Flanagan in February 2008 has highlighted this as being a major concern. Paperwork is a problem that affects many leaders. A fairly simple way of organizing your time in respect of paperwork that flows over your desk is to ask yourself a few questions about the item in question. Table 4.1 illustrates what is meant by this approach.

Table 4.1 Choices about paperwork

Question	Action
What would happen if I did nothing?	If the answer is 'nothing', then dispose of it accordingly.
Can I delegate this?	If you can, then do so.
Can I deal with it now?	If you can, then do so.
Do I need to find out more?	If you do, then take the necessary action to get more information.

4.10 Decision-Making and the Stages Involved

Police leaders, particularly supervisors, have to make decisions and take actions that seriously affect other human beings. Often these decisions have to be made spontaneously, with little time to consider the major implications of them. However, this decision may be the subject of evaluation by others either as colleagues, other supervisors, or even the courts. It is therefore important that the decision that is made is correct most of the time as individual's rights may be affected.

Decisions are often merely problem-solving exercises. The process involved in solving problems is as follows:

- recognizing the problem;
- gathering the necessary information;
- developing suitable solutions;
- analysing suitable solutions;
- selecting a correct solution.

We will examine these in a little more detail in the following section.

4.10.1 **Recognizing the problem**

Do you know the problem that you are trying to resolve? This is a fundamental point—you need to be as clear as possible about what you are trying to do. Without this, the whole job of decision-making is like a house built on sand. It will eventually fall down! If you aren't sure about what you are trying to resolve, try writing it down, leave it for a short time and then take another look at it. By doing this, you are almost certain to refocus about what you are trying to resolve.

4.10.2. **Gathering the necessary information**

Once you have decided what the problem is, the next step is to gather all the necessary information, and sorting it into something meaningful. Sometimes all of the information you need will be immediately available and clearly seen, but sometimes other information may be missing. It is an important point to note at this stage that decisions made without all of the available information are not generally good decisions. There is also a difference between available and relevant information. A question you need to ask yourself when considering all information available to you is this: **Is this information relevant to my decision?**

The two types of information are shown below in Figure 4.2.

Of course, within the modern police service there is an enormous amount of management information available for leaders to make a decision upon. However, this highlights a dilemma: the managerialist approach means that people have access to more and more data, in order to make decisions, but the large number of sources for this information makes it very difficult to keep up with the latest knowledge!

Also, let us suppose that the information overlap as illustrated in Figure 4.2 above is not sufficient for your needs. What is your next course of action? Well,

Figure 4.2 Types of information

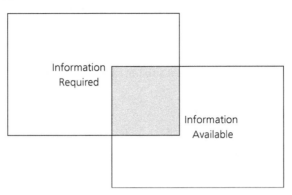

you start by trying to get more information, but obtaining this by doing research can be timely and costly. Therefore, you will reach a point when you have to make a decision on all the available data you have. In general, though, you will find that you acquire a great deal of information in a relatively short time, sufficient for you to make a well-informed and correct decision.

4.10.3 Developing suitable solutions

Supervisors who lack skill in this area tend to make decisions far too quickly and end up with just one or two solutions. They tend not to give enough time and thought to considering three or four possible solutions. It is at this point that the leader needs to have an open mind and the ability to think around problems and consider all possibilities. Creative thinking is a valuable asset here. Your solutions, however, must be feasible, or capable of being carried out or realized. For example, as a supervisor you may have to provide a solution to incidents of anti-social behaviour occurring in an area that has low unemployment. Perhaps your solutions to the problem would include the increase of jobs in that area. However, is it feasible that you alone can provide that solution? The answer is that in all probability you cannot. You have to be realistic in your attempts at providing solutions to specific problems.

4.10.4 Analysing the solutions

What makes decisions difficult is the problem of risk. 'Looking before you leap' is a useful proverb to remember when considering decisions and there is skill involved in working out risks. A useful way of considering or analysing your solutions is to think of what would happen in the worst case scenario. Can you accept the worse case scenario or would it be too much for you to contemplate? Once you have thought through this aspect you will need to analyse the worse case scenario and do all you can to reduce the risk. Here, experience, practice, consultation with staff and others, and mental rehearsals are all relevant in analysing whether the solution will be the right one.

4.10.5 Selecting a correct decision

Once you have undergone the above process, it is time to select a correct decision from your feasible solutions. First you need to establish selection criteria. A useful way of doing this is to divide your requirements into three specific areas. Figure 4.3 below shows you in schematic form the criteria involved.

Figure 4.3 The criteria used when selecting decisions

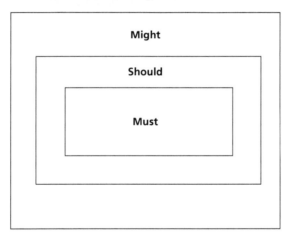

Unless your option meets all the MUST requirements the capable leader should discard it. However, once all the essential requirements have been met, the list of SHOULDS and MIGHTS may come into play

For more complex decisions you might employ one or more of the following methods:

- List the advantages and disadvantages of the decision.
- Examine the results of each course of action.
- Test the decision against the aims and objectives of the task.
- Weigh up the risks against the expected gains.

4.11 Involving Others in Decision-Making

A good supervisor, as a leader, has to realize that he/she has to have the support of the people they lead. In order to do this, a leader needs their commitment and this means involving people in the stages of the decision-making process.

Remember that the more people are involved in the decision-making process that ultimately impacts upon their working lives, the more motivated they will be in carrying out the decisions. However, the way in which you as a leader can share decision-making will differ according to the situation you find yourself in. For example, you may find yourself with plenty of time to come up with a solution and you can consult for a long period. However, there may be some occasions when you need to make an instant decision because of time constraints. This will obviously affect your ability to consult with people. However, whenever possible, a good leader will utilize their staff. Some important questions a leader will need to consider in this process can be seen in the Key Point box below.

KEY POINT—CHECKLIST OF USEFUL QUESTIONS IN UTILISING STAFF

- Have I agreed the aims and objectives with the team?
- Have the team been involved in collecting all the information required?
- Has the team been involved in generating a number of feasible options?
- Has the consensus of the team been tested in the introduction of possible options?
- Has everyone shown commitment to the solution?

4.12 **Indecision**

Indecision, or the inability to decide or problem solve, causes anxiety and frustration for both the decision-maker and fellow workers. People will have no confidence in a leader who is not decisive. This could be disastrous where, in a stressful situation, police personnel need to be instructed quickly in order to carry out their function without hesitation. Whilst people may criticize a wrong decision, they will certainly criticize a leader who makes no decision.

Leaders are paid to make decisions. These can be divided into three broad types, namely:

- Routine or everyday decisions which mean responding to predictable needs such as providing staff for pre-planned events.
- Emergency decisions which require precise responses in a crisis, such as the deployment of staff to functions to deal with a serious incident
- Significant decisions which will affect other people and resources which require quite a lot of research and judgement before a decision is reached.

4.13 **Decision-Making Checklist**

- Where a decision is urgent and important—**make it!**
- Where the decision is important and you have time available to consider your options, take that time.

• Explain to others that you are taking time because of the complexity of the problem and impose a time limit on your solution.

4.14 **Communicating Decisions**

Once you have made your decision, you need to communicate it. You have to tell people what you have decided because, as a leader, communication is a vital skill. Within the police organization your decisions may become part of the operating procedures, such as how a particular police operation will be carried out. Sometimes the decisions will result in change in the way a system is carried out and will become part of a new system.

Remember that communication must be all embracing if it is to be effective. There are people who work within the police organization who may be part-time staff, or involved in job share through family friendly policies. Special constables, who are important elements in all forms of policing, may need to be communicated to. This aspect of your decision-making needs to be carefully thought through to ensure everyone involved receives the information.

4.15 **Following Up your Decision**

Sometimes during the consultation and application process of a decision, there may be resistance to the decision in some quarters. This is often seen when comments such as 'the latest idea from the leisure deck' or the 'latest fad' is used to describe the decision. Leaders should not be surprised at this resistance as many see new ideas as a threat. Despite the fact that consultation is very important it is a fact of life that you will not be able to consult with everyone on all the decisions you make. Further, some decisions as already stated, will need to be made quickly which will mean a minimum of consultation available.

Assessing the outcomes of your decision process is useful and will feed back into any future decision-making process. A useful way of doing this is by using an outcome window, as shown in Figure 4.4 below.

Using this approach the leader can assess the impact of the decision in both a positive and negative effects and also on the leader and others. Now that we know about the outcomes box, read Exercise 4E below and fill in an outcomes box to assess the impact of the decision in the two possible results shown.

EXERCISE 4E Assessing the impact of decisions

You are the leader of a neighbourhood policing team and you are informed that there has been a rise in graffiti offences in a particular area of your neighbourhood. These seem to be occurring during late nights at the weekend. You decide to have your team work late shift on Friday and Saturday evenings until the culprit(s) are caught.

What are the possible outcomes in the following results:
1. The culprit is caught on the first evening.
2. The culprit is never caught.

Figure 4.4 The outcomes box

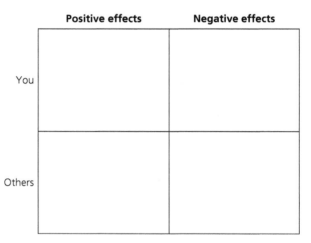

4.16 **Conclusion**

Clearly, an effective leader needs to be visible and interactive with their staff. People expect a lot from those who are in charge and leaders need to understand that their personal approach to the workplace is very influential on how their colleagues view then as leaders and motivators. Winning respect, confidence, and loyalty of the staff they lead should be of paramount importance and much of this can be achieved by being decisive and caring about the development of the individual staff member.

4.17 **Summing Up**

4.17.1 **The main qualities that staff look for in a police leader**

- Being committed to achieving a high quality service to the community and supporting staff to achieve this.
- Displaying high personal and professional standards and challenging poor behaviour.

- Enabling, valuing, and developing staff.
- Having relevant knowledge and skills.

4.16.2 **Being a better leader and administrator**

A person can become a better leader and administrator if they:

- identify as many of their own shortcomings as possible and work to improve them. This requires an honest and reflective approach to thinking about oneself;
- practice their leadership characteristics as much as possible. This could be patience, being decisive, being approachable etc;
- put in the time and effort required but practice will improve performance as a supervisor. As a leader one may have to sell oneself to others, and one way of doing this is to gain respect.

4.16.3 **Winning respect is an important part of police leadership**

This is achieved by the following:

- encouraging staff to speak freely;
- keeping up to date with professional knowledge;
- acknowledging good work with praise;
- being consistent;
- displaying high levels of personal integrity;
- being professional.

4.16.4 **Loyalty**

Loyalty is essentially an emotional feeling rather than an intellectual commitment. It is not one sided and people who are led will only feel loyal to their leaders if the leader is loyal to them.

4.16.5 **Morale**

The morale of people in the workplace should be one of the most important considerations of any leader. Morale is not something that is easily identified, but simply means the zeal, enthusiasm, or belief which underpins a person's or group's work or task.

4.16.6 **Developing individuals**

Leaders and supervisors need to understand that part of leading from the front is their role in developing those individuals whom they work with or are part of their team. Developing individuals does not always mean formal training courses for people although these are vital. Sometimes on-the-job training is an effective way of developing people, and this can be done in the main by coaching or mentoring.

4.16.7 **The definition of coaching**

Coaching is helping and supporting people to manage their own learning and maximizing their potential to develop their skills and improve their performance.

4.16.8 **Mentoring**

Mentoring includes coaching, facilitating, counselling, and networking. The mentor not only shows an individual how to do a job, but also provides encouragement and shares enthusiasm for the job in hand. Whilst coaching is an enabling and helping process, mentoring is more of a supportive role.

4.16.8 **Time management**

A skilled leader should be able to manage their own time. If one cannot organize oneself, how can one organize anyone or anything else? Time keeping and time management is a priority for any leader.

4.16.9 **The problem-solving process**

The problem-solving process involves the following:

- recognising a problem;
- gathering the necessary information;
- developing suitable solutions;
- analysing suitable solutions;
- selecting a correct solution.

4.16.10 **Decision-making**

Police leaders, particularly supervisors, have to make decisions and take actions that seriously affect other human beings.

4.16.11 **Indecision**

Indecision, or the inability to decide or problem solve, causes anxiety and frustration for both the decision-maker and fellow workers. People will have no confidence in a leader who is not decisive. This could be disastrous where, in a stressful situation, police personnel need to be instructed quickly in order to carry out their function without hesitation.

References and Further Reading

Dobby, J., Anscombe, J. and Tuffin R. (2004) *Police Leadership: Expectations and Impact,* London: Home Office.

Janis, I.L. (1982) Groupthink: *Psychological Studies of Policy Decisions and Fiascos,* Boston, MA, USA: Houghton Mifflin Company.

Melnicoe, W.B. and Mennig, J.C. (2002) *Elements of Police Supervision,* California, USA: Glencoe Publishing.

Northouse, P.G. (2006) *Leadership: Theory and Practice,* Middlesex: Sage.

Parsloe, E. (2004) *The Manager as Coach and Mentor,* Trowbridge: Cromwell Press.

Useful websites

Free website on creative leadership available at <http://www.ccl.org/leadership/index. aspx>.

National Policing Improvement Agency available at <http://www.npia.police.uk/en/ index.htm>.

The Flanagan Report on Policing available at <http://police.homeoffice.gov.uk/news-and-publications/publication/police-reform/Review_of_policing_final_report/>.

SPACE FOR NOTES

SPACE FOR NOTES

SPACE FOR NOTES

SPACE FOR NOTES

Ethical Leadership

5.1 **Introduction**

Leaders are people who are an example to others regarding the right way to do something and the right way to behave. As a leader, people whom you are responsible for will look to you for that example and for the correct guidance and advice. If the police service is to acquire a professional status then that advice must be correct and appropriate and non-discriminatory. It must also be ethical as ethical behaviour underpins a professional approach to the way a person carries out their job. It is also necessary to understand the idea of people as being customers if the police are to successfully adopt an ethical approach to dealing with members of the community. Also, the police leader needs to understand what have been the main drivers for the application of ethical policing, the legislative framework that underpins workplace philosophy, and how the Police Code of Conduct applies along with the work of the Independent Police Complaints Commission. This chapter discusses these major issues.

5.2 **Customers**

The idea that people who come into contact with the police should be afforded the status of a customer is an idea that is common throughout this book. It is easy for people when they come into contact with others to place them into certain recognizable categories. By doing so they feel they are able to respond accordingly in an approved organizational manner. For example, people sometimes 'stereotype' others according to their accent, religion, or skin colour. Further, the police tend to categorize people as victims, witnesses, offenders, and so on and they then deal with them according to whatever category the police place them in. The problem is that this sometimes leads to people not being dealt with as they should be, but are dealt with as perhaps a victim of a crime who may be from a poor area. This can sometimes mean that the person, although a victim of crime, may not be treated as they should be because of the area they live in.

If the police regard everyone they deal with as a customer then this problem may be overcome as dealing with them this way will ensure their approach is the correct one. Customers can be internal, that is people who work within the police organization, and external, that is people who are victims, witnesses, even offenders. Treating people as customers is an underpinning philosophy if the police service is to be regarded as a true profession.

Furthermore, we must remember that customers provide the police with information that can be processed into useful intelligence. This intelligence is used to support the National Intelligence Model and intelligence-led policing that underpins much of today's policing philosophy.

It is believed that information from customers can be used to tackle all forms of crime and disorder, including terrorism. If the police deal with people professionally and courteously as customers should be, then the community will be more likely to support the police in their endeavours. However, the police need not only to deal with their customers in that way, but also in a manner that puts them beyond reproach. They must be ethical.

5.3 **Ethics**

First, try the following exercise.

EXERCISE 5A What do we mean by Ethics?

Write down what you think ethics actually means.

One definition of ethics is simply put as how police officers and police leaders make the right judgements and do the right things for the right reasons (Neyroud and Buckley 2001). This is a simple, yet effective definition. It is about doing the right thing.

The police are a powerful organization and agents of the Crown. For example, one definition of policing includes the legitimate use of coercive force within the boundary of the State (Klockars 1999). Currently, there are more armed police officers in Great Britain than ever before and the use of TASERS, the electronic 'gun' that incapacitates a person by allowing an electronic current to run through them, are being piloted across the country. Police staff can, in certain, justified circumstances, kill people. Therefore this authority should be used in a fair and non-arbitrary way.

There is in fact a 'trade off' between the police organization and the public. The public expect the police to behave in a manner that protects each individual's rights within the law, but they also expect fair treatment in their dealings with them when they turn to them for help.

Ethics is closely linked with the idea of integrity. As a leader within the police organization a person should always behave ethically and with integrity. Integrity means being trustworthy and honest; it is about being clear what the police service stands for and always behaving in accordance with those values as guides.

5.3.1 **Police officer discretion**

Earlier, it was stated that ethics was doing the right thing. However, doing the right thing does not amount to doing the same thing in all circumstances. Some people may think that the police enforce every breach of the law. Imagine the outcry and attitude towards the police if this happened no matter how small or insignificant the breach. It is not an officer's duty to indiscriminately prosecute every person who commits an offence. Under the idea of consensual policing, police officers have an obligation to balance, and if possible reconcile conflicting views in the interests of the community as a whole.

As long as the police are seen to act in good faith, it remains their prerogative not to investigate complaints but just to record them. This exercise of discretion is recognized as an essential policing skill.

Discretion can be understood as:

- freedom of judgement and action;
- the authority to decide and choose;
- selecting the best course of action, having recognized and considered all of the alternatives.

However, where discretion is used in the operation of police powers the rights of an individual may be affected. By using discretion an officer will sometimes be making a decision not to act in circumstances where it may seem that their duty as a constable requires them to act. Failure to act could be interpreted as favouring or discriminating against certain individuals or groups which can lead to accusations of neglect of duty, harassment, or corruption. Therefore, a police officer must make sure that the decisions they make are fair. A key component of an officer's decision-making will be their personal and professional integrity.

5.4 Policing a Complex Society

British society is comprised of different communities and these communities may themselves be sub-divided into smaller groups. Neither these communities nor groups are exclusive as it is possible for an individual to be a member of various communities or various groups. Some of these sections in society may be identified as vulnerable with particular needs. In addition, there may be tensions that exist between certain groups and some of them will have different perceptions of the police. It is important to realize that the attitude and behaviour of one individual police officer may enhance or diminish community trust. A good point to remember is that every contact leaves a trace, which is a phrase borrowed from forensic science. It reinforces the idea that how you deal with a person influences their perception of not only you as an individual, but also the organization you represent. Whilst thinking about communities and what they are made up of, try the following exercise.

EXERCISE 5B Make up of communities

(a) Make a list of the identifiable groups within the community where you live.

(b) From this list, identify which of these groups are vulnerable and include your reasons for this.

Police officers, like all people, have a 'frame of reference' or 'way of seeing the world' which is influenced by many factors, including the community or groups to which they belong. Other factors that impact on an individuals' 'frame of reference' could include their education, religion, family and upbringing, or cultural background. These factors are responsible for developing a person's values and their prejudices. This is shown in Figure 5.1.

Figure 5.1 How a frame of reference is developed

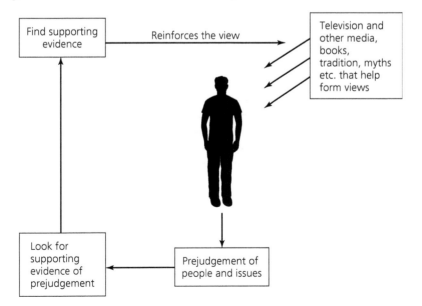

EXERCISE 5C

Using the information above and also the cycle of subjectivity, consider your attitudes to the following groups:

1. Travellers
2. Unemployed people
3. Immigrants

Reflect upon where your attitudes come from and how these influence your own values.

By analysing this and placing ourselves in the cycle, we may be able to identify the source of our values, recognise our personal prejudices and then challenge our perceptions of any unfamiliar or minority groups in our community. This forces us to think about how our own values affect our attitudes and behaviour and then consider the impact that these attitudes and behaviour might have on others. Try completing Exercise 5C above and see if you can identify where some of your values and attitudes have come from and how they may influence your views of people or groups.

5.5 **Prejudice and Discrimination**

5.5.1 **Prejudice**

EXERCISE 5D What does prejudice mean to you?

What do you think of when you hear the word prejudice?

Prejudice can be defined as making negative pre-judgements about other people or other groups. Prejudice may be suppressed, but it may often come out in our underlying attitudes, opinions, and beliefs. Most people join the police organization with some prejudice, which they may or may not be aware of. Our prejudices often stem from relying on our 'frame of reference' or subjective views to fill in the gaps in our knowledge of other groups in society. This is where *stereotyping* becomes predominant. Stereotyping is about making sweeping generalizations about groups of people, where you believe that just because people are members of a particular group, they must, because of that fact, share particular traits which you think are characteristic of that group.

Consider the information contained in the following exercise.

EXERCISE 5E Media and stereotypes

A national newspaper reports that the increase in crime is all down to the fact that we have a record number of immigrants in the country.

Reflect upon this statement. Do you consider that there are some generalizations or stereotyping at work here?

If a person is aware of their prejudices they can start to challenge their validity. By questioning why you think like that, you can work on changing your views and attitudes.

On way of understanding how prejudice can work, particularly within the workplace, is to look at the work of Gordon Allport (1979). Whilst Allport's work was initially about trying to understand why Nazi Germany dealt with the Jewish population in the way it did, his work can be relevant to how people suffer prejudice in contemporary society. Gordon Allport explained that prejudice can follow a discernible pattern and that if not challenged an individual can experience each level which gets progressively worse over time. The various stages are explained below.

- *Anti-Locution*—Could be demonstrated by using phrases of colour which equate whiteness with purity and blackness to bad or evil. Other examples are using stereotypical language or ethnic jokes.
- *Avoidance*—Quite simply this means to avoid another individual or group.
- *Discrimination*—Means unequal treatment. This unequal treatment reinforces the power of the dominant group and disadvantages the minority group. Discrimination on the grounds of religion, gender, sexual orientation, disability, and age are unlawful. The process of discrimination can include denying employment or less professional service delivery.
- *Physical Attacks*—These may range from attacks on the property of the individuals to direct physical attacks.
- *Extermination*—This is the ultimate violent expression of a prejudice. On an extreme level this could be demonstrated by the ethnic cleansing of a whole community. Within an organization this could be interpreted as forcing someone to leave an employment position, or forcing a family to move out of a particular estate or area.

Allport's ideas showing the stages a person can travel through when suffering prejudice can be seen in Figure 5.2 below.

Figure 5.2 Allport's scale of anti-locution

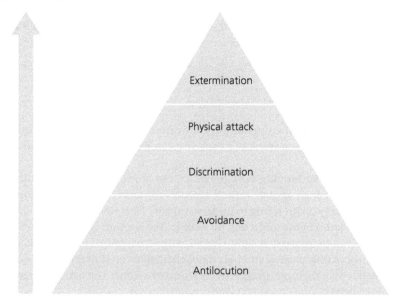

Extermination

Physical attack

Discrimination

Avoidance

Antilocution

5.5.2 **Discrimination**

The importance of understanding the nature and presence of prejudice lies in the fact that when an individual has power and is prejudiced they are in a position to discriminate against others. Discrimination occurs when someone acts more favourably towards one group of people or an individual than another and that favouritism is based on prejudice and has no justification.

Discrimination is normally seen in four main ways. Leaders need to understand the way in which discrimination can occur in the workplace, and must be able to challenge it accordingly.

(i) *Direct discrimination* occurs when a person treats one person or a group of people less favourably than another person or group in similar circumstances. Examples include:

- only searching individuals from a particular ethnic minority group;
- ignoring bullying in the workplace;
- assuming that all Asians are terrorists and therefore applying handcuffs to all Asians who are arrested no matter what the circumstances.

(ii) *Indirect discrimination* means selection criteria, policies, benefits, employment rules, or any other practices which, although they are applied to all employees, have the effect of putting some individuals at a disadvantage. An example would be an employer who imposes a requirement that all employees must have short hair may put people of a certain religious belief at a disadvantage when compared with other employees. This type of discrimination is unlawful whether it is intentional or not.

(iii) *Positive discrimination* is also unlawful. For example, a position becomes available for a firearms officer in a particular police force. A female and an Asian male apply and the supervisor selects the Asian male as he/she wishes to have more ethnic minority officers within the department despite the fact that he is less well qualified for the position than the female. This is positive discrimination for the Asian male but is negative discrimination against the female. Opposed to this, there may be a situation where there is a need for 'positive action'. 'Positive action' means doing something to prevent or compensate for disadvantages experienced by individuals in a certain group. This is allowed in two areas:

- access to training and educational facilities; or
- to encourage people to take up employment opportunities.

This means employers are able to target their recruitment advertising at individuals from minority groups, as long as the position itself is open to all.

(iv) *Victimization* is a type of discrimination whereby a person is discriminated against because they have made allegations of discrimination under, perhaps, employment legislation outlined in this chapter. It is aimed at protecting a person who has made a complaint or brought a case under this legislation or any person who has given evidence or information in connection with proceedings. Such victimization is often aimed at dissuading the person from pursuing their grievance.

Individuals who suffer discrimination are victims and must be regarded as such. The trauma individuals suffer because of discrimination is at best unpleasant, while for some it is devastating, affecting their mental and physical well-being in the long term. Bearing this in mind, complete Exercise 5F below.

EXERCISE 5F

Try to imagine that you have been the victim of discrimination. Spend a few minutes reflecting on how you might feel.

You may have included some of the following:

- guilt as a victim that it was your fault;
- mistrust of the police;
- anger at being treated differently;
- humiliation and distress;
- isolation;
- feeling of further victimisation.

5.6 **Institutional Racism**

The Scarman Report following the Brixton riots of 1981 highlighted a loss of confidence in the police and policing methods. It was during Lord Scarman's inquiry that the issue of 'institutional racism' was first raised. The Scarman Inquiry was set up to examine the strained relationship between police and some members of the black community. Relations had deteriorated when, following a significant increase in street crime in Lambeth, operation 'Swamp 81' was launched. The consequences were that a disproportionate number of black youths were stopped and searched, intensifying the resentment of this group. Violence broke out with 299 police officers injured and at least 65 civilians. Petrol bombs were thrown for the first time in mainland Britain and 82 arrests were made. As a result of these riots the Home Secretary appointed Lord Scarman to hold a public inquiry. Scarman identified evidence of 'racial prejudice' in the behaviour of certain officers who acted out their personal prejudices.

Despite this report, some years later the McPherson Inquiry into the investigation of the murder of the black teenager Stephen Lawrence again revealed officers with unacceptable attitudes. On 22 April 1993 Stephen Lawrence was murdered in a racist incident in London. In a 1997 inquest Mrs Lawrence publicly accused the police of handling the initial investigation badly, stereotyping Stephen as a criminal and treating the family insensitively.

In 1999 McPherson published his report. There were a number of findings, most of which were highly critical of police action. The McPherson Report sought to explain the incompetent police investigation into Stephen Lawrence's murder by the existence of 'institutional racism' in the Metropolitan Police Service. During the inquiry it became apparent that a form of racism was being displayed by some investigating officers who failed to recognize the attack as 'racist' from the start which inevitably hampered the investigation. This failure was attributed to 'unwitting' racism, which is defined as making certain assumptions about individuals on the basis of generalized information, or usually misinformation.

A number of recommendations were made as a result of the McPherson Inquiry. Recommendation 69 stated that 'all police officers and civilian staff should be trained in racism awareness and valuing cultural diversity'. Further recommendations were also made in relation to recruitment and retention with the proposal that policing plans include targets for recruitment, retention, and progression of ethnic minority staff. Most importantly the inquiry provided a definition of 'institutional racism' which can be seen in the following Key Point box.

> **KEY POINT—DEFINITION OF INSTITUTIONAL RACISM**
>
> The collective failure of an organization to provide an appropriate and professional service to people because of their colour, culture, or ethnic origin. It can be seen or detected in processes, attitudes, and behaviour which amount to discrimination through unwitting prejudice, ignorance, thoughtlessness, and racist stereotyping which disadvantage minority ethnic people.

The use of the phrase 'unwitting' highlighted that there had been an unintended disadvantage to ethnic minorities. The concept of institutional racism recognizes that an organization may not *intend* to act in a racist way, but that its structures or its culture means that patterns of recruitment, promotion, or service delivery may result in people from racial minorities being disadvantaged. For example, many of the policies and procedures may have been written many years go and not updated to appreciate the needs and requirements of a modern diverse British society. Therefore, it is important to understand that institutional racism is not unique to the police. Society as a whole faces these challenges and every individual and institution has a responsibility to examine their behaviour and prejudices.

5.7 Identifying a Racist, Homophobic Incident, or Hate Crime

As a leader, you will need to be sensitive to the issues of race and diversity. Identifying a racist, homophobic, or hate crime offence is of great importance.

5.7.1 Hate crimes

Definition of hate crime

Any crime where the perpetrator's prejudice against any identifiable group of people is a factor in determining who is victimized.

Therefore, a victim of hate crime does not have to be a member of a minority group or someone who is generally considered to be 'vulnerable'. Effectively anyone can be the victim of a hate crime incident.

5.7.2 **Racist incident**

Definition of a racist incident

The McPherson Report discussed above defined a racist incident as: 'any incident which is perceived to be racist by the victim or any other person'.

The recording of racist incidents is therefore now based on the perception by *any* person that the incident is racist. 'Racist' does not simply relate to colour, but also to race, nationality, ethnic, religious, or national origins.

5.7.3 **Homophobic incident**

'Homophobic' does not only relate to lesbian women, gay men, bisexuals, transgender, or transsexual people, but to any person perceived to be so by the perpetrator. As with racist incidents, the recording of homophobic incidents is based on the perception by any person that the incident is homophobic. The person making the report does not need to have any evidence to show that the incident was racist or homophobic. If any person believes that the incident was so motivated, it must be recorded as such.

It appears that under-reporting remains a common feature of all these types of crimes as victims may be reluctant to report the incident to the police. It has also further been identified that many victims have suffered repeated problems before they contact the police. It is important to appreciate why victims are reluctant to contact the police. Exercise 5G below helps you to reflect upon this.

EXERCISE 5G Why people don't report racist or hate crimes

Write down some reasons why the victim of a racist/homophobic incident or hate crime may be reluctant to report the incident to the police.

The impact of this type of crime can be more traumatic on the victim due to the realization that a normally impersonal crime is actually a personal attack. As well as affecting the individual, hate crime is considered as a powerful poison to society as it breeds suspicion, mistrust, alienation, and fear. In this present climate of heightened tension following the recent terrorist attacks, racists frequently exploit periods of raised anxiety and therefore there needs to be a heightened state of alert for hate crime with prompt action against racial harassment and strong support and reassurance for victims.

5.8 **The Police Code of Conduct**

The framework for how police officers should carry out their job is contained in the Police Code of Conduct which is found in Schedule 1 to the Police (Conduct) Regulations 2004. These regulations apply to *all* police officers including special constables. The main areas covered by this code can be seen below along with a brief explanation of their impact upon the conduct required.

- Honesty and integrity—It is important that the public has faith in the honesty and integrity of police officers, and as such officers should be open and truthful in all their dealings.
- Fairness and impartiality—Police officers have a responsibility to act with fairness and impartiality in their dealings with everyone.
- Politeness and tolerance—Officers should treat members of the public and colleagues with courtesy and respect, avoiding abusive or deriding attitudes or behaviour.
- Use of force and abuse of authority—Officers must never knowingly use more force than is reasonable, nor should they abuse their authority.
- Performance of duties—Officers should be conscientious and diligent in the performance of their duties. Officers should attend work promptly when rostered for duty and if unable to work through sickness or injury, they should avoid activities likely to retard their return to duty.
- Lawful orders—The police service is a disciplined body and unless there is good and sufficient cause to do otherwise, officers must obey all lawful orders and abide by the provisions of Police Regulations.
- Confidentiality—Information which comes into the possession of the police should be treated as confidential and it should not be used for personal benefit and nor should it be divulged to other parties except in the proper course of police duty.
- Criminal offences—Officers must report any proceedings for a criminal offence taken against them as conviction of a criminal offence of itself results in further action being taken.
- Property—Officers must exercise reasonable care to prevent loss or damage to property.
- Sobriety—Whilst on duty officers must be sober and should not consume alcohol unless specifically authorized to do so or it becomes necessary for the proper discharge of police duty.
- Appearance—Unless on duties which dictate otherwise, officers should always be well turned out, clean and tidy whilst on duty in uniform or in plain clothes.
- General conduct—Whether on or off duty, police officers should not behave in a way which is likely to bring discredit upon the police service.

5.9 **The Work of the Independent Police Complaints Commission**

The Independent Police Complaints Commission (IPCC) became operational on 1 April 2004. It is a Non-Departmental Public Body (NDPB), funded by the Home Office, but by a law entirely independent of the police, interest groups, and political parties and whose decisions on cases are free from government involvement. The IPCC have a legal duty to oversee the whole of the police complaints system, created by the Police Reform Act 2002, and their aim is to transform the way in which complaints against the police are handled.

The Police Reform Act 2002 sets out the statutory powers and responsibilities of the IPCC, Chief Police Officers, and Police Authorities for the new complaints system. This guarantees the independence of the Commission, outlines its role as guardian of the police complaints system as a whole, and gives the IPCC a duty to raise public confidence.

The IPCC has a wide range of new, stronger powers to radically change the way complaints against the police are handled in England and Wales. The IPCC can choose to manage or supervise the police investigation into a case and independently investigate the most serious cases.

A complaint can be made by a member of the public who:

- has been the victim of misconduct by a person serving with the police. Misconduct could include a police officer or member of police staff being rude to a member of the public or using excessive force. It could also include unlawful arrest or an abuse of human rights;
- was present when the alleged misconduct took place, or close enough to see or hear the misconduct, and as a result suffered loss, damage, distress or inconvenience, or was put in danger or at risk;
- is a friend or relative of the victim of the alleged misconduct, distressed by the effects of the incident on the victim;
- has witnessed the alleged misconduct;
- is acting on behalf of any of the above. However, a person who wants someone to complain on their behalf must give their consent in writing.

5.9.1 **Complaints and conduct matters**

When a leader or supervisor has to consider complaints it means they have to separate complaints from different matters relating to police conduct. There are three quite specific types that leaders need to understand when it comes to these issues. These types are:

- complaints;
- conduct matters, or death and serious injury matters; and
- recordable conduct matters.

These will be discussed briefly below.

Complaints

Part 2 of the Police Reform Act 2002 defines complaints as:

- Any complaint about the conduct of a person serving with the police. This means a sworn constable, an employee under the direction or control of a chief officer or a special constable.
- The complaint will amount to a Part 2 complaint where it is made, in writing or otherwise, by:
  - a member of the public who claims to be the person in relation to whom the conduct took place; or
  - a member of the public who claims to have been adversely affected by the conduct or to have witnessed the conduct; or
  - any person acting on behalf of any of the above.

KEY POINT—RELEVANT PERSON MAKING A COMPLAINT

The relevant person has to be physically present nearby when the conduct took place and was able to see or hear conduct or the effects of it in order to make a Part 2 complaint. So a person hearing information from a third party, or someone seeing something on television will not be sufficient for a person to make a complaint under this section.

Conduct matters and death and serious injury matters

The first thing to understand is the definition of a 'conduct matter'. This in general relates to any matter which is not and has not been the subject of a complaint but there is an indication that a person serving with the police may have committed a criminal offence or behaved in a manner which would justify the instigation of disciplinary proceedings.

A death or serious injury matter is any circumstances whereby a person died or suffered serious injury whereby the following requirements are met:

- The deceased or person seriously injured had been arrested by a person serving with the police and had not been released or otherwise detained in custody.
- At or before the time of death or serious injury the person had contact, either direct or indirect, with a person serving with the police who was acting in the execution of their duty, and there is indication that the contact may have caused or contributed to the death or serious injury.

Recordable conduct matters

The complaints framework allows for the recording of complaints where an officer has ceased to serve with the police and also for recording complaints where the identity of the officer is unknown.

A recordable conduct matter means:

- a conduct matter that is required to be recorded by the appropriate authority or has so been recorded; or
- any matter brought to the attention of the appropriate authority under that sub-paragraph.

5.9.2 Dealing with complaints, conduct matters, and DSI matters

The provisions for dealing with such matters can be found in Part 2 of the Act and also in Schedule 3 to the Police Reform Act 2002.

Table 5.1 below illustrates the requirements under this schedule.

Table 5.1 Requirements under Schedule 3 to the Police Reform Act 2002

Details	Responsible body	Action required
Complaint made about conduct of a chief officer	Police Authority	All steps are taken initially and from time to time, to obtain and preserve evidence relating to the conduct complained of.
Complaint made about the conduct of a person under the direction and control of a chief officer	chief officer	1. Take appropriate steps for obtaining and preserving evidence relating to the conduct complained of. 2. It is the duty of a chief officer to take all specific steps for obtaining or preserving evidence relating to the conduct that is the subject of a complaint as directed by the Police Authority for the area in question.

KEY POINT—OBLIGATION TO PRESERVE EVIDENCE

These provisions place an obligation upon the Police Authority and the chief officer to obtain and preserve relevant evidence. This duty is a continuing duty and may be reviewed from time to time.

5.9.3 The referral of complaints to the IPCC

There are occasions where complaints must be referred to the IPCC. However, there are occasions where the referral of complaints may be left to the discretion of the appropriate authority.

Mandatory complaints, those that must be referred to the IPCC, include:

- Where the complaint is one that alleges that the conduct resulted in the death or serious injury of someone.
- The complaint is one that is a specified complaint, namely
  i. a serious assault, a serious sexual offence, or serious corruption;
  ii. a criminal offence or behaviour which is liable to lead to a disciplinary offence but is aggravated by discrimination on the grounds of a person's race, sex, religion, or other status;
  iii. an offence for which the sentence is fixed by law, or an offence for which a person of 18 years or over could be sentenced to seven years' imprisonment or more.

Voluntary complaints are those that the appropriate authority considers that it would be appropriate to refer them because of:

- the gravity of the subject-matter of the complaint; or
- any exceptional circumstances.

Sometimes, because of the nature of the complaint the IPCC can notify the appropriate authority that it requires the complaint in question to be referred to it for consideration.

5.9.4 The IPCC and its investigations

When the IPCC has decided that an investigation is necessary, the IPCC has to decide the form that the investigation must take, having regard to the seriousness of the allegation and the public interest. Table 5.2 below illustrates the different levels of investigation.

Table 5.2 Levels of investigation and IPCC involvement

Level	IPCC involvement
One	An investigation carried out by the appropriate authority itself on its own behalf.
Two	Supervised investigations whereby the IPCC supervise and liaise closely with the Investigating Officer. The difference between this level and level one is that the IPCC has considerable power and discretion regarding the Investigating Officer and the Investigating Officer must comply with all requirements imposed by the IPCC.
Three	These investigations are carried out by the appropriate authority but are actively managed by the IPCC. In managed investigations, the Investigating Officer is under the direction and control of the IPCC, and the submission of any report is directly to the IPCC, a copy being provided to the appropriate authority.
Four	This is the highest level of independent investigation available into reported police misconduct. These investigations, which are a new concept for the police service, involve the appointment of an IPCC member as the Investigating Officer, along with such others as are thought necessary to assist in the investigation.

5.10 **Significant Events**

Several important events have lead to the introduction of ideas underpinning the ethical approach to policing, and these in turn have an effect upon the way leaders in the police organization should behave. They are worthy of some understanding and are discussed below.

5.10.1 **The ACPO Statement of Common Purpose**

A major impact upon the drive for ethical policing can be seen in the Statement of Common Purpose issued by the Association of Chief Police Officers (ACPO). This statement underpins much of the way in which the police organization carries out its function. The statement says that the purpose of the police is:

- to uphold the law fairly and firmly;
- to prevent crime;
- to pursue and bring to justice those who break the law;
- to keep the Queen's peace;
- to protect, help, and reassure the community;
- to be seen to do all this with integrity, common sense, and sound judgement.

It also reinforces the fact that officers must be compassionate, courteous, and patient, acting without fear or favour or prejudice to the rights of others.

5.10.2 **The Human Rights Act 1998**

The implications of the police not acting fairly, ethically, and with integrity can be significant. This is because the police are a powerful organization and they have the opportunity to breach the rights of individuals. The Human Rights Act 1998 has provided new avenues for the public to challenge unethical activities of public bodies including the police. It also has placed responsibility on these public bodies to ensure that their actions are compatible with the European Convention on Human Rights. It places a responsibility to safeguard citizen's rights and freedoms on every police employee in the UK.

5.10.3 **Public enquiries**

In recent years there have been some significant public inquiries that have provided a driver for change in the way the police do their job. Many of these public enquiries have criticized police culture and methods of working, and also police values and ethics. Despite the fact that they make an initial negative impact on public perceptions of the service and damage the integrity of the police, these inquiries have played a large part in forming and changing police policy, procedures, practices, and legislation. Three in particular are worthy of deeper consideration.

The Scarman Inquiry was set up in 1981 to examine the strained relationship between the police and some areas of the black community. Relations had deteriorated following the launching of operation 'Swamp 81'. The consequence of this operation was that a significant and disproportionate number of black youths were stopped and searched, intensifying the resentment of this group towards the police. Following the subsequent riots in Brixton, Lord Scarman's public inquiry made it clear that the riot was a result of an outburst of violence against the police. Some of the recommendations that came out of the Scarman report are:

- to eliminate prejudice from the force by improving police training;
- a reform of the complaints procedure to secure public confidence.

The report into the murder of Stephen Lawrence has been described as a 'landmark in the history of policing and race relations in this country'. The Macpherson Report was published as a result of an inquiry into the investigation of the murder. There were a number of findings, most of which were highly critical of the police action at the scene of the murder and during the subsequent investigation. Recommendations were made as a result. Some of these recommendations had training implications, such as Commendation 69 which states that 'all police officers and civilian staff should be trained in racism awareness and valuing cultural diversity'.

The brutal murder of eight-year-old Victoria Climbie was one of the worst cases of child abuse Britain has ever seen. The subsequent report into her death identified that neither of the two constables who dealt with the investigation were trained detectives. The report stated that 'all police officers should, as a result of their initial training, be aware of the basic principles of effective investigation'. It was further recommended that the Home Office must devise and implement a national training curriculum for child protection officers.

5.10.4 **Partnership policing**

Since the introduction of the Crime and Disorder Act 1998 and the recent review of that Act the emphasis of much police activity lies in the partnership approach to policing (see Rogers 2006). The police are now only one of the organizations with a remit to improve levels of safety and reassurance. Partnerships between the police and other bodies, particularly local authorities and community groups are vital aspects of policing. Section 17 of the Crime and Disorder Act 1998 imposes an obligation on every police authority, local authority, and other specified bodies to consider crime and disorder reduction in the exercise of all their duties. Increasing participation in policing is seen as a potential way of improving police professional practice. This means that the police organization is exposed to more interaction with other professional bodies than ever before and must be seen to act ethically and with integrity when working with them.

5.11 **Legislative Framework**

Leaders within the police organization need to understand the legislative framework that underpins the workplace within which they operate. This means having at least a basic knowledge of laws that influence employment. They exist to prohibit discrimination and protect the rights of various groups, both within the workplace and in society as a whole. It is important that all police staff are aware of this aspect of the law and that they are aware of the obligations it places upon police forces.

5.11.1 **Sex Discrimination Act 1975**

The provisions of the Sex Discrimination Act 1975 make it illegal to treat a woman or a man less favourably on the grounds of their sex or marital status in the areas of employment, training and education, and the provision of goods, facilities, and services to members of the public. The Act also makes sexual harassment unlawful. Sexual harassment is unwanted, unreciprocated, and offensive conduct imposed on another person because of his or her sex.

EXERCISE 5H What is sexual harassment?

What types of behaviour do you consider to be sexual harassment?

You may have thought of the following:

- sexual harassment can involve physical contact ranging from unnecessary touching through to more serious types of physical assault;
- verbal, suggestive remarks, 'jokes', sexual propositions, unwanted comments;
- verbal abuse of a sexual nature;
- it could also include wolf whistles or displaying or circulating sexually explicit material.

It is important to note that the offending behaviour may not be targeted at an individual but could consist of a general culture which, for instance, appears to tolerate sexist jokes.

5.11.2 **The Race Relations Act 1976**

This Act makes it unlawful to discriminate against others on the grounds of race in relation to certain areas, namely employment, training and education, and the provision of goods, facilities and services. Under the 1976 Act Chief Officers of police were held not to be vicariously liable for the discriminatory behaviour of their officers. This situation was amended with the Race Relations Act 2000.

5.11.3 **The Race Relations Act 2000**

This Act extended the 1976 Act to include the police service and the rest of the public. It clearly prohibits the police from discriminating—directly, indirectly or by victimization—in carrying out their policing functions. It also created a duty on all public authorities to promote equality of opportunity and good relations between persons of different racial groups. Every public authority, including the police, therefore has to put in place means to ensure that their internal organization is fair to ethnic minorities and that in the delivery of their services they pay attention to race issues.

5.11.4 **The Disability Discrimination Act 1995**

This Act introduced a relatively new area of discrimination, that of disability. The Act introduces a statutory right not to be discriminated against on grounds of disability. Employers are placed under a duty to make 'reasonable adjustments' to working conditions or physical features within the workplace where these would place a disabled person at a 'substantial disadvantage'. Examples of the duty to make reasonable adjustments would include adapting keyboards or providing laptop computers and adapting access points to buildings.

5.11.5 **The Disability Discrimination Act 2005**

This Act both extended and amended the 1995 Act. There is now a duty on public authorities to ensure better performance in relation to eliminating disability discrimination. New groups were added who can now also benefit from the Act's protection, including those who have cancer, HIV infection, or Multiple Sclerosis.

5.11.6 **The Employment Equality (Age) Regulations 2006**

This legislation ensures that employers can no longer discriminate against employees on the grounds of age unless it can be objectively justified. An example of age discrimination could occur when a young person employed by the police is continuously informed that they are too young to know anything and they find this behaviour humiliating and distressing. There may be certain circumstances when employers can justify discriminating on the grounds of age, but they have to prove that it is a proportionate way of achieving a legitimate aim. Proportionate means that what the employer is doing has to be appropriate and necessary. An employer might argue that it was appropriate and necessary to refuse to recruit people over 60 where there is a long and expensive training period before starting the job. In this case, the legitimate aim would be the need for a person to be in a job for a reasonable period before they retire, and for the employer to see a return on the investment they have put into training the employee. The employer would have to show that there was no less discriminatory way of achieving the aim.

5.12 **Summing Up**

5.12.1 **Consumers**

The consumer of the products and services of an organization, often called the external customer, and everyone within the organization who is in effect an 'internal customer'.

5.12.2 **Ethics**

One definition of ethics is simply how police officers and police leaders make the right judgements and do the right things for the right reasons.

5.12.3 **Prejudice**

Prejudice can be defined as making negative pre-judgements about other people or other groups. Prejudice may be suppressed, but it may often come out in our underlying attitudes, opinions, and beliefs.

5.12.4 **Discrimination**

Discrimination is normally seen in four main ways:

- *Direct discrimination*—occurs when a person treats one person or a group of people less favourably than another person or group in similar circumstances.
- *Indirect discrimination*—means selection criteria, policies, benefits, employment rules, or any other practices which, although they are applied to all employees, have the effect of putting some individuals at a disadvantage.
- *Positive discrimination*—is also unlawful. For example, a position becomes available for a firearms officer in a particular police force.
- *Victimisation*—is a type of discrimination whereby a person is discriminated against because they have made allegations of discrimination under, perhaps, employment legislation outlined in this chapter.

5.12.5 **Institutional racism**

Institutional racism is defined as;

> The collective failure of an organization to provide an appropriate and professional service to people because of their colour, culture or ethnic origin. It can be seen or detected in processes, attitudes and behaviour which amount to discrimination through unwitting prejudice, ignorance, thoughtlessness and racist stereotyping which disadvantage ethnic minority people.

5.12.6 **Hate crimes**

Hate crimes are defined as;

> Any crime where the perpetrator's prejudice against any identifiable group
> of people is a factor in determining who is victimised.

5.12.7 **Racist incident**

The McPherson Report defined a racist incident as 'any incident which is
perceived to be racist by the victim or any other person'.

5.12.8 **The Independent Police Complaints Commission**

The Independent Police Complaints Commission (IPCC) became operational
on 1 April 2004. It is a Non-Departmental Public Body (NDPB), funded by the
Home Office, but by law entirely independent of the police, interest groups,
and political parties and whose decisions on cases are free from government
involvement.

5.12.9 **The ACPO Statement of Common Purpose**

A major impact upon the drive for ethical policing can be seen in the
Statement of Common Purpose issued by the Association of Chief Police
Officers (ACPO). This statement underpins much of the way in which the
police organization carries out its function. The statement says that the purpose of the police is:

- to uphold the law fairly and firmly;
- to prevent crime;
- to pursue and bring to justice those who break the law;
- to keep the Queen's peace;
- to protect, help and reassure the community;
- to be seen to do all this with integrity, common sense, and sound
  judgement.

5.12.10 **The Scarman Inquiry**

The Scarman Inquiry was set up in 1981 to examine the strained relationship
between the police and some areas of the black community. Relations had
deteriorated following the launching of operation 'Swamp 81'.

5.12.11 **The Macpherson Report**

The report into the murder of Stephen Lawrence has been described as a 'landmark in the history of policing and race relations in this country'. The Macpherson Report was published as a result of an inquiry into the investigation of the murder.

References and Further Reading

Allport, G.W. (1979) *The Nature of Prejudice*, USA: Perseus Books.

Clements, P. (2006) *Policing a Diverse Society*, Oxford: Oxford University Press.

Klockars, C.B. (1985) *The Idea of Police*, London: Sage.

Neyroud P. and Buckley A. (2001) *Policing, Ethics and Human Rights*, Cullompton: Willan.

Miller, S., Blackler, J. and Alexandra, A. (2006) *Police Ethics*, Australia: Allen and Unwin.

Useful websites

The Independent Police Complaints Commission available at <http://www.ipcc.gov.uk/>.

The association of Chief Police Officers available at <http://www.acpo.police.uk/>.

Home Office website on police ethics available at <http://www.homeoffice.gov.uk/rds/policeethics.html>.

A useful website that examines all aspects of prejudice available at <http://www.understandingprejudice.org/>.

The McPherson Report available at <http://www.archive.official-documents.co.uk/document/cm42/4262/4262.htm>.

SPACE FOR NOTES

SPACE FOR NOTES

SPACE FOR NOTES

Meetings

6.1 **Introduction**

It is said that the ideal meeting is two people, with one absent! However, if there is one thing that is a mixed blessing, it is meetings. The police service in England and Wales is an organization that depends upon the efforts of staff to achieve any measure of success. Information sharing is a vital part of this process, especially now the fact that it is not the sole responsibility of the police alone to tackle crime and disorder has been established. As part of the information sharing process, and indeed the consultation process between police and community, meetings are a crucial element of police business. Police staff need to have the skills and abilities to handle meetings, whether as a participant or indeed as the chairperson. This chapter will explain why meetings are necessary and how to successfully take part in them.

6.2 **Meeting Customers' Needs**

One of the main reasons why the police engage in meetings is to ensure that the service they provide meets the needs of the customers they serve. The idea of the police service having to satisfy customers is a relatively new one, yet in reality the police have always had customers. This idea can be problematic for some people. Consider what you think the term 'customer' means and answer the question in Exercise 6A below.

EXERCISE 6A

What do you think the term 'customer' actually means? Write your answer on a separate sheet of paper.

Definition of the term 'customer' as used in this book

The consumer of the products and services of an organization, often called the 'external customer', and everyone within the organization who is in effect an 'internal customer'.

'Internal customers' mean those people that the police employee works with day after day and has regular contact with. 'External customers' are those who use the services provided by the police. The difference is, of course, that for some customers the service provided by the police may be unwelcome, such as a police officer arresting an individual for committing an offence of burglary. Even so, the suspect in this case is still a recipient of policing services and will be dealt with according to the rule of law as outlined by the Police and Criminal Evidence Act 1984.

6.2.1 **Why is customer care important?**

Apart from the fact that as an individual employee of the police you should behave in the most professional manner at all times, there are some important points that you need to understand about satisfied customers. These are:

- A satisfied customer causes less stress to the individual. Having to deal with a dissatisfied customer can induce much stress to you when having to sort out problems caused by others.
- Satisfied customers take up less of your time, as having to deal with complaints and problems is very time-consuming.
- A person who is satisfied with they way they have been dealt with will tell others about it and this can only help promote a positive image of the police.
- As a professional you will gain enormous pleasure from satisfying customers and this will motivate yourself and the people who work with you.
- It is sometimes difficult to remember, but customers are human beings and it should be natural to want to provide a good service to them. How would you feel if a close member of your family was not treated with courtesy by the police organization?

6.3 **Partnerships and Community Together Meetings**

Perhaps the one type of meeting that members of the extended policing family are likely to encounter is the meeting known as Partnerships and Community Together (PACT) meetings. PACT is the name given to the neighbourhood meetings that will form the structure through which Neighborhood Policing will be delivered.

It is anticipated that PACT meetings will develop into a forum where the partnerships that serve a neighbourhood are tasked with tackling the problems of crime and disorder identified by the community. They will take place within every neighbourhood approximately once a month in order to deal with the issues that affect residents. They should be attended by members of every section of that neighbourhood and, in theory at least, be managed by neighbourhood residents. Partners will be tasked by and responsible to the PACT meeting for working with the community members and groups to resolve the identified issues. Initially, it is envisaged that these meetings will be organized and managed by the police.

6.3.1 **What are the benefits of PACT meetings?**

The benefits for the police and partnerships in engaging in this consultation process can be summarized as follows:

- It gives a structure that will deliver the main requirements for Neighbourhood Policing to be effective.

- It is about delivering community engagement.
- It is about problem-solving policing of low-level localized policing and partnership issues.
- It is about gathering community intelligence.
- It means giving everyone the chance to see members of their neighbourhood team in person at least once per month.
- It is about communicating with local people and telling them what their neighbourhood team is doing for them.

In terms of structure these meetings should be publicized during the last two weeks of every month in key locations. Further, they should:

- take place during the first week of every month;
- take place immediately after the meeting and be open to those who have attended the meeting;
- initially comprise members of the public who have attended the meeting and partners who can take action to deal with the priorities;
- be developed over time by the neighbourhood team and the public so that the panel is comprised only of members of the public who task the neighbourhood team on behalf of the meeting;
- enable people to task their local police officer and other partners in their own neighbourhoods;
- identify up to three top partnership priorities at a community level every month.

6.4 **The Importance of Meetings**

Unfortunately, many people consider meetings a big waste of time and unproductive. When you consider that a large amount of time is spent by people attending meetings during their working days, you realize the importance of learning and using effective meeting skills.

A meeting is a discussion involving two or more people and has six main functions which are shown below:

- They provide an opportunity for exchanges to take place quickly.
- They provide an environment whereby people can offer new ideas.
- They lessen some of the difficulties encountered in face-to-face meetings.
- People who attend meetings are more likely to become committed to new ideas.
- They increase teamwork and can empower individuals.
- They are used to explain why things are happening and provide an opportunity to answer questions.

Meetings therefore play an important part in the working lives of all police personnel and are an important facet when trying to achieve objectives. Make a list of the meetings you have recently attended.

Some of the meetings you may have thought of could include:

- team/relief/sector meetings;
- BCU management meetings;
- operational user (eg custody officer) groups;
- planning meetings;
- staff meetings;
- health and safety meetings;
- staff development meetings.

The reality is the list could go on. The important point is they all need to be run effectively if they are to have the best impact.

6.5 Costs and Benefits of Meetings

Meetings mean that people are removed from their normal daily activities for a specific purpose. Therefore, we could say that there is an immediate cost implication for the individuals and the organization in that they are away from normal service delivery to the customer and away from helping to achieve the organization's aims and objectives. However, benefits of attendance at a meeting could be an increase in awareness of issues surrounding service delivery, such as crime and disorder problems, which could mean an enhanced service delivery as a result of the meeting. This is just one example.

EXERCISE 6B Costs and benefits of holding meetings

List what you think may be the costs and benefits of holding meetings. The first line has been done for you as an example.

Costs	Benefits
They waste time	They are informative

You may have considered some of the following in your answers:	
They waste money	Problems are analysed and solved
They slow down progress	Feedback is sought and obtained
They breed office politics	People are motivated
They exclude others	Aims and objectives are clearly identified

Having identified the fact that there may be costs and benefits attached to holding meetings, we need to consider how best to remove or at least minimize the costs and maximize the benefits. To do this we need to consider several important points. These are:

- Is the meeting really necessary?
- Regular meetings.
- The agenda.
- Why are we meeting?
- Time and timing.
- The people.
- The meeting environment.

These will be examined in a little more detail.

6.6 Is the Meeting Really Necessary?

This really is an important question to ask when considering setting up a meeting. There may be other ways of dealing with the business in hand. An important consideration in this is whether the meeting is one that you have called, or, if it is not your meeting, whether or not it needs to be attended. If it is your meeting, then you need to pause and reflect. Is your meeting a debate or consultation? Can a decision be made without these? Can the information be disseminated any other way? If all that is required is a quick chat with someone in the corridor or on the telephone then maybe this is the best way to progress an issue. As soon as you reflect in this manner, alternatives start to present themselves and it may be that less time can be spent trying to achieve an objective.

However, on many occasions, you may have to attend meetings called by others. Of course, there will always be some meetings that you have to attend, but you can still reflect upon your attendance for others. There may be some meetings that you attend for the wrong reasons, such as being there just in case something is introduced into the meeting that may interest you, or to see someone for personal reasons. Sometimes, as a leader, you may need to delegate attendance to others to act as your representative and to report back to you and, of course, if you need to know what went on, you can always read the minutes of the meeting. Minutes are a record of a meeting which can be used to prompt action, identify who is responsible for what, and the timescales involved. They can also be used later on to justify action taken or show the official record of what took place at the meeting.

Whatever the meeting, you need to make sure that it is essential and that no alternative to holding it is feasible.

KEY POINT—WHAT ARE MINUTES OF A MEETING?

Minutes are a record of a meeting which can be used to prompt action, identify who is responsible for what, and the timescales involved. It can also be used later on to justify action taken or show the official record of what took place at the meeting.

6.6.1 **Regular meetings**

If it is important to consider whether or not a single meeting is necessary, then it is much more important when thinking about holding and being committed to a series of regular meetings, such as weekly or monthly. Sometimes these meetings are held just out of habit and no other real reason, and if that is the case then there is no doubt that they are not really useful. However, the advantage of a fixed schedule of meetings lies in the fact that often a person can plan ahead in terms of their diary and know their commitments in advance. That said, it is sometimes better to think in terms of '10 a year' rather than one a month because of some of the variations that occur for individuals during 12 months, such as courses or annual leave. This means of course that at different times of the year, some meetings will be closer together than others. Regular meetings can of course be cancelled, although there may be a temptation to let them be held on the basis of seeing who turns up and who says what. Remember that this approach may earn you a reputation as a leader who runs meaningless meetings!

6.6.2 **The agenda**

Every meeting needs to have an agenda. An agenda is a list of things to be done, or in the case of meetings items of business to be considered. In most cases this needs to be in writing and circulated well in advance. Whilst this is a basic point, there are occasions when it is not done, and this leads to an ineffective meeting. A clear agenda is needed to provide 'shape' and control in all sorts of ways. It should:

- specify the formalities, such as the need to note apologies from those unable to attend;
- link to points and issues from previous meetings to ensure continuity;

129

- give people the chance to offer amendments to the agenda;
- specify who will lead or contribute to each item;
- help individuals to prepare for their input into the meeting;
- order the items for discussion or review and they should be in a logical order of the topics.

KEY POINT—WHAT IS AN AGENDA?

An agenda is a list of things to be done, or in the case of meetings items of business to be considered.

The sequence of the agenda is also very important. Order selection can make all the difference and it is best to consider all the items using the following criteria:

- Is the item one that needs to be dealt with very early whilst people are fresh?
- Is the item one that needs to be placed so as to link with others?
- Is the item one that needs a lot of preparation?
- Is the item interesting and important to everyone or just one or two?
- Is the item one that will take too much time?

Above all, an agenda needs to be realistic. For a start, it will need to fit the time available for the meeting. Will one major item overshadow the rest of the items? Are the right people present for the items on the agenda?

A good leader in charge of a meeting will check the agenda for balance and the overall style or look. Above all, the agenda should reflect the objectives of the meeting. An example of a simple agenda can be seen in Figure 6.1

6.6.3 **Why are we meeting?**

Sometimes meetings are not effective because of how they proceed—they are ineffective from the start because they do not have clear specific objectives. The setting of clear explicit objectives is vital, so a good leader needs to think long and hard about this aspect of meetings. If objectives are clear they can help run meetings in a number of ways such as:

- people will understand why the meeting is taking place;
- people will be better prepared and more likely to participate;
- the discussion will be more focused;
- the proceedings will be easier to control.

If this simple rule is observed, the meeting is more likely to achieve its aims.

Figure 6.1 A simple agenda

> ## ANYTOWN NEIGHBOURHOOD POLICING TEAM
> ## AGENDA FOR MEETING TO IMPROVE DETECTION RATES
> ### Time, date and place
>
> **No. Item**
>
> 1. **Attendance and apologies to be noted.** *(Secretary to note)*
>
> 2. **Minutes of previous meetings.** *(Discussed and if agreed passed as being a true and accurate record)*
>
> 3. **Correspondence received.** *(Secretary to inform meeting)*
>
> 4. **Updates from previous actions.** *(Input by those tasked at last meeting with results from specific actions)*
>
> 5. **Monthly crime statistics.** *(Input by Crime Analyst)*
>
> 6. **Monthly update on performance figures.** *(Input by member of BCU management team)*
>
> 7. **Staffing levels.** *(Chairperson)*
>
> 8. **Any other business.** *(This usually relates to something discussed in this meeting, **NOT** a new item that should be placed on the agenda)*
>
> 9. **Time, date and location of next meeting.** *(Minutes of meeting to be circulated two weeks before next meeting).*

6.7 **Effective Meetings**

Probably everyone has attended a meeting at some time. Think for a moment about meetings you have attended and it is certain that you will identify some that appeared to have no structure or were not well run. Leaders in the police service need to be able to run meetings with staff, customers, and others in as effective a manner as possible. Before reading on try Exercise 6C below.

> ### EXERCISE 6C Positive and negative experiences of meetings
>
> Think of a recent meeting you have attended. Write down what you consider to be the positive things and the negative things about that meeting. Reflect upon how the meeting could have been more effective.

Meetings should have a purpose and that is to make sure that action is taken. In very broad terms, therefore, a meeting should:

- have a purpose;
- achieve its purpose;

- take only as much time as necessary;
- involve only the people who need to be there;
- result in action, not words.

Compare this list with what you wrote down in the above exercise. Can you see any similarity between your meeting and some of the purposes of a meeting?

6.8 Informal Meetings

Informal meetings can take several different forms and are often very useful places for people to discuss issues. Whether they occur by chance or are organized in an informal manner, such as by word of mouth, they should be viewed as an opportunity to resolve many issues. Informal meetings, irrespective of their casual nature, can benefit from well-chosen surroundings. People will engage with you more freely if they feel comfortable and it must be remembered that the right surroundings are very important.

Impromptu meetings occur at very short notice and can occur at any time. It may be that passing someone in the corridor can prompt a brief meeting between two people and they are ideal for discussing things frankly and for reaching a decision quickly. However, they are probably best used to resolve minor issues and should never really involve more than three or four people. Sometimes this type of meeting is used for urgent announcements and they tend to be more relaxed with a more casual language style and relaxed body language.

Small informal meetings are very useful for discussing, problem-solving, and giving feedback. If they are planned they allow for preparation time, which is not the case with impromptu or 'off-the-cuff' type meetings. It is important to remember that even though these meetings may contain a small number of people, the purpose of the meeting should always be borne in mind and this means they will remain focused and not overrun in terms of time.

6.9 Effective Control of Meetings

Good effective meetings are those that achieve their aims and objectives within agreed timescales. These meetings keep direction, and usually have well thought out agendas which are not too long or complicated. There are several areas that need to be considered before the meeting, including thinking ahead in order to plan effectively. Once a clear agenda has been formulated and prepared it will need to be circulated as previously discussed.

Many of the problems that arise in meetings can be avoided by good preparation and participation by all those in attendance. In particular, one should always:

- study all the material that has been circulated before the meeting;
- start and finish on time;

- stick to the agenda at all times;
- make sure that everyone involved in the meeting is fully aware of any decisions that have been made;
- ensure, especially if you are the chairperson, that as many people as possible are involved in any question and answer session.

Usually at the end of a meeting there is an agenda item called 'any other business'. If you are chairing a meeting it is important to allow people to have their say here but do so by imposing an orderly approach. Your meeting could be spoiled at this stage by a number of people talking at once or engaging in arguments over points not on the agenda.

6.10 **Leading a Meeting**

Every meeting needs to have a person who is responsible for running and controlling it. Normally this person is called the 'chairperson' or 'chair'. A person who is a good chairperson will ensure that the meeting is well-directed, which in turn means that the meeting will be focused better on its objectives, discussions will be more constructive, and that all sides of an argument or viewpoint can be reflected upon and considered. Further, the meeting can be maintained in a businesslike and less argumentative manner. A good leader of meetings, for that is what a chairperson is, will handle the discussions and see that objectives are met promptly, efficiently, effectively, and without wasting time.

Leading a meeting, therefore, means a person needs to use genuine skills that need to be learned and practised. Consider the skills you think a good leader needs to have to run a meeting and attempt the following exercise.

EXERCISE 6D

Write down a list of the skills required by a leader of meetings.

You may have thought of some of the following in your list above:

- must have the respect of all those attending;
- come to the meeting prepared;
- be on time and start the meeting on time;
- ensure that matters such as refreshments, minute-taking etc. are arranged;
- start on a positive and correct note smoothly leading into the agenda;
- introduce people to each other if necessary;
- set and keep to the rules for the meeting such as allowing only one person to speak at a time;
- ask questions to clarify matters not only for yourself but making sure others in the meeting understand the points made;

- keep the meeting on course for its objectives;
- deal professionally with outbursts and sudden displays of emotion;
- summarize discussions and provide the final word bringing matters to a conclusion;
- ensure that any action points allocated to individuals are clear with appropriate time scales for action.

A good leader of meetings will be able to achieve these things without really being aware they are doing so, but they must be achieved with humour, patience, and respect for all those present.

6.11 **Starting the Meeting**

The better type of meeting starts off well, then continues well and ends well. A good start to the meeting is therefore essential as it helps set the scene and atmosphere for the remainder of the meeting. This is the responsibility of the leader or chair of the meeting. A good way to start the meeting is to:

- be positive;
- ensure everyone understands the purpose of the meeting;
- create the right atmosphere;
- encourage interest and enthusiasm for what is to come;
- encourage a business-like approach.

It also helps if the leader or chair involves others early on in the meeting rather than beginning with a lengthy introduction. Prompting discussion is an important skill to master for the person leading a meeting.

6.11.1 **Prompting discussion**

First, try the following exercise.

EXERCISE 6E

Think about times where you have attended a meeting. The meeting could be anywhere about anything. Did you feel inhibited from taking part? Were there occasions when you wanted to take part but did not?

Write down the reasons why you think people are reluctant to be involved in discussions during meetings.

Part of the leader's skills includes encouraging individuals to take part in discussions. To ensure that adequate and representative discussion is achieved, and also to ensure that adequate decisions are reached on all the available information, the leader or chairperson needs to prompt discussion from everyone. Sometimes there are specific reasons why people attending meetings do not participate fully. In the exercise you were asked to consider this. You may have thought of the following:

- fear of rejection or ridicule about their views or opinions;
- feeling pressure from other, perhaps more senior, people present;
- lack of adequate preparation;
- not having an understanding of what has gone before.

Sometimes a person may just lack encouragement to engage in the discussion process. A good chair will ask for views and do so in a manner that promotes open and considered comments. Often, promoting comments and discussions will occur by the method of asking those present questions and these questions should be clear and easily understood by all present. There are two kinds of questions, namely open and closed questions.

6.11.2 **Open questions**

These are questions that cannot be answered with a simple 'yes' or 'no' as they require the person answering the question to provide a little more thought in their responses. These questions are more likely to get people talking and generally start with the words 'What', 'Why', and 'How' and are best introduced as part of a phrase such as 'Tell me about . . .' or 'What do you think about . . .?'.

6.11.3 **Closed questions**

This type of question is useful when the leader does not wish to encourage more talk about a subject. Closed questions can be answered with a simple 'yes' or 'no' or in some other brief response.

Prompting discussion is as important as controlling the meeting. It is often the only way of ensuring that the meeting is well-balanced and can take into account the many views of those present. If decisions are made in the absence of prompting, you as leader or chair of the meeting may be criticized later for not taking into account the views of people who may say that they never really got a chance to put their point of view across.

In order to makes sure that this does not happen, the leader of the meeting has to make sure that all comments available are obtained. This can be done in a number of ways, but the following examples are useful:

- Asking the question again. Re-phrasing the question, to make sure perhaps that everyone understands what was said and to ensure that the point is clear and that people realize that a response is required from them.

- Using silence. Even a short silence can be sufficient to get someone to speak. Therefore, after asking your question, do not rush onto something else, as the silence may be enough to obtain a response.

6.12 **Disruption in Meetings**

Sometimes, because of the topic or aims of a meeting, people can become emotionally involved and this can lead to disruption or even disorder within the meeting. There are some key rules for the person leading the meeting in these circumatances. These are:

- Never get upset or emotional yourself, no matter how hard this may be.
- Isolate one aspect of what is being discussed and deal with that in a way that reduces the overall emotion of the debate.
- Show sympathy with the sentiments being expressed before re-consolidating the meeting. This can be achieved by a simple phrase such as 'The point you have raised is important and bound to influence our emotions. Let's take one issue at a time . . .'.

More often than not this approach will work to defuse a situation, but if it does not work then as the leader of the meeting you can take a stronger approach such as calling for a short break and insisting that it is taken with no further discussion about the controversial subject. For a leader to abandon a meeting must clearly be a last resort, but as such it may be better to do so than allow a disorderly meeting to continue.

6.13 **People**

People vary in their attitudes and approaches to many different things. Meetings therefore can often comprise of people who have different personal styles and this may sometimes be viewed as a mis-match. The first time to consider this is when contemplating who should attend the meeting, although in reality we sometimes have very little control of attendees at meetings. What we may consider as unfortunate combinations are sometimes inevitable, but there are ways of practically dealing with difficult people. Forsyth (2001) has provided a typology of 'difficult' people and how to deal with them in the context of meetings. This is shown in Table 6.1 below.

Table 6.1 Dealing with difficult people

Category	Details	Response
The Talkative	Often these people are show-offs who want attention, but on a positive side can be enthusiastic. Tries to monopolize discussions and overpower others.	Get a word in, call a halt to the flow of words with a positive comment such as 'thanks'. Move on and ask the group a question based on what was said by the talkative person.
The Gusher	This person is intent on drowning out others and getting their point over at the expense of others.	Timed agenda and good discipline will help here. Concentrate on a single point the gusher has made and turn the discussion towards other members of the meeting.
The Sphinx	People who remain silent are also a problem, especially if you know they have valuable contributions to make.	Asking questions is the best tactic here. Sometimes you may need to ask simple questions with more complex follow-up questions to get the person more involved.
Separate Meeters	These people engage in whispered conversations throughout the meeting and can be distracting.	Pausing isolates the distraction and draws attention to them. You can also ask a question of them to determine if what they are whispering about is relevant to the meeting.
Chip on Shoulder	This person has a particular problem or grievance and sees the meeting as the place to air it.	Be specific with the individual and ask them to refer back to the original reason for the meeting. If appropriate promise to look at the problem at another time, but get the meeting back on track.
The Devious	Many people may not say what they really feel or mean. What people say may underplay, overstate, or disguise the facts.	This is difficult, but you must try to read between the lines of what is being said. Good minute-taking will ensure what is said is faithfully recorded for future reference.
The Aggressive Bully	Some people will try and force their way over everything including rules and normal accepted behaviour to get their own way.	This needs firm action without undue delay. The rules need to be laid down and use the rest of the group in the meeting to back you up.

Source: Adapted from Forsyth (2001) 55–57.

The responsibilities of a person leading a meeting is summarized in Figure 6.2 below.

Figure 6.2 Responsibilities of leading a meeting

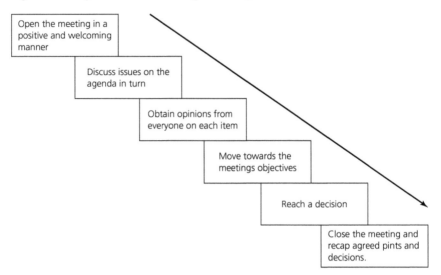

6.14 **Personal Development Review Meetings with Staff**

6.14.1 **Introduction**

The system of annual meetings between supervisors and staff used to be called a staff appraisal. However, staff appraisals tended to concentrate on past performance and paid little attention to future development of staff or even continuous professional development of individuals. Therefore the system of Performance and Development Review (PDR) is now intended to be a continuous process which improves motivation, skills, and abilities and also to encourage the best possible performances from people, whatever job they are carrying out for the organization. By doing so, it is believed that this will lead to improvements within the whole organization. By doing what is needed in the right way benefits not just the individual but the whole of the police organization and ultimately the public and community. Whilst the PDR does assess past performance too, its intention is to use the assessment to identify ways of improving performance for the future. The differences between the old staff appraisal and the PDR approach can be summarized as follows:

• PDR focuses on how things are achieved, not just on what has been achieved.
• PDR is used to improve the image of the police organization to the customers.

- PDR moves the focus for meetings from the past to the future by using objectives for the next 12 months.

The whole process is continuous in nature and can be seen in Figure 6.3 below.

Figure 6.3 The PDR process

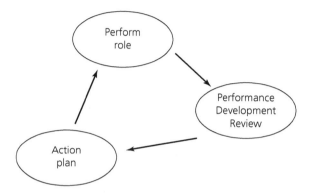

6.14.2 **The stages of a Performance Development Review**

The stages that the review undergoes are summarized in Table 6.2 below:

Table 6.2 Stages of a Performance Development Review

Stage	Action
Team member prepares for meeting	Assesses past performance against current role requirements and previous action plans, identifies possible future plans.
Supervisor prepares for meeting	Assesses team member's past performance and identifies forces and local objectives to which team member should contribute.
The meeting itself	Four parts, namely: i. review of team members' performance; ii. establishing and agreeing role requirement for the future; iii. discussing and agreeing development needs which will fill in skills and experience gaps; iv. agreeing a record which can be used in the future.

6.14.3 **Staff portfolio of evidence**

It can be difficult to assess your own performance and provide evidence of your achievements if you are a team member about to engage in the PDR process. This can only be done if you keep sufficient records, such as a portfolio of evidence. This should contain a 'preparation form' or something similar which allows a person to plan effectively for their PDR meeting.

The form may look something like the example shown in Figure 6.4 below.

Figure 6.4 PDR preparation form

PDR Preparation Form

Staff

Part A: Reviewing the past 12 months.

i.   With regard to your agreed list of priorities, what do you think you have achieved?

ii. How could this performance have been improved?

iii. Reflect upon how effective any training or development activities you have undertaken have been.

Part B: Planning for the next 12 months.

List the policing priorities you intend to focus on?

What additional responsibilities would you like to take on in your current role?

What further experience would you like to obtain?

What training or development would you like to receive for your current or future roles?

6.14.4 **Preparation by the supervisor**

There are two main steps for the supervisor to work through before the meeting. These are as follows:

1. Assess the actual performance of the team member in a number of skill areas and compare them with the priorities set during previous performance and development reviews and against the requirements for the actual role occupied by the person.
2. Think about local policing priorities and objectives, with a view to ensuring that the training and development needs of the staff member are compatible with them.

For the supervisor there are some very important points to remember when dealing with these types of meetings. The meeting is used to assess a person's performance in the workplace so the supervisor must remember a number of important points before the meeting takes place. These are:

- All assessments must be based upon evidence, not gossip, innuendo, or feelings.
- The core skills of an individual will need consideration, such as professional and ethical standards, communication, self-motivation, decision-making, creativity, and innovation.
- The assessment must be free of bias, prejudice, and discrimination.
- The supervisor must be aware of the problems as relying on stereotyping or first impressions.

Following the review, having knowledge of force and individual requirements, the supervisor and the staff member should attempt to agree on an action plan for the next 12 months. This is sometimes called a role requirement.

6.14.5 **The role requirement**

Role requirements show how the work of each individual can contribute towards the achievement of their objectives. They identify the key tasks of a person's job and set priorities and therefore are based upon the job description or force/departmental plans. The role requirement should be a document that precisely identifies what an individual should be doing. It should really have two main parts to it. These are:

1. A summary of the most important tasks, containing two or more important areas which the team member should concentrate on. These should reflect force priorities.
2. A statement of priorities and objectives linked to police strategies and plans, and agreed by the team member and the manager.

Consider the following example in the following Key Point box.

KEY POINT—ROLE REQUIREMENT

You are a supervisor in charge of a neighbourhood policing team. One of your team members is responsible for a particular area that has suffered from a large amount of anti-social behaviour involving youths.

1. Your force wants to encourage community cohesion by involving the implementation of diversionary activities for youths. This is also a local priority.
2. Your team is responsible for dealing with anti-social behaviour calls where youths are allegedly involved.

> 3. Your team member works very closely with schools in the area.
> 4. As part of the role requirement, the supervisor and team member may agree that he/she should have a specific objective of assisting local residents in forming a youth club with activities for the youth in the area.

Consider the scenario above about role requirements. Do you think that the objective or agreement between the supervisor and the team member is:

- Realistic?
- Achievable?
- Measurable?
- Fair?

This is an important point. Objectives agreed between supervisors and team members need to be effective, and for that to occur they need to be SMARTER. It is possible that you know about this type of objective setting. In the context of the personal development process this mnemonic stands for:

S	**Specific**	precisely-worded and accurate
M	**Measurable**	the word 'better' cannot be measured whereas a percentage can be
A	**Achievable**	it needs to be within the person's ability and range
R	**Relevant**	to the needs of the force and wishes of the individual
T	**Time constrained**	setting a time when progress will be reviewed

In particular in terms of the PDR process they should also:

E	**Enhance performance**
R	**Raise standards**

Attempt the following exercise and see if you can identify if anything is wrong with the objectives.

EXERCISE 6F Objectives

A. To lead more effectively.
B. To be more accurate when reporting on staff sickness.
C. To submit every report on the day before it is due to be submitted.
D. To study bricklaying.
E. To complete an interview course.

You may have thought of some of these as your answers to the particular objectives:

1. Not specific.
2. Cannot be measured as 'more' is not defined quantitatively.
3. Probably not achievable.
4. Not relevant for policing needs.
5. Is not time constrained.

6.14.6 Development of staff

Following the stages of a PDR, the supervisor and the team member are now in a position to include staff development within the action plan. This identifies how the team member will achieve the objectives stated in the role requirement. Remember that training and education of staff should be regarded as an *investment*, not an abstraction from the workplace. For example, an objective in a role requirement might be concerned with presentation skills. An action plan may therefore include a number of options for a person to improve in this area such as:

- attending a short presentation skills course;
- coaching from an experienced colleague;
- constructive feedback from colleagues following presentations.

There are many ways in which individuals can increase their skills levels and improve their performance in the workplace. Action plans could include some of the following:

- formal training courses including in-force courses, external short courses, and longer-term educational programmes at universities and colleges;
- self-managed learning including reflective practice upon experiences, continuous personal development, role modelling, and tutor work;
- using others around you for constructive feedback, coaching, mentoring, secondments, and shadowing others;
- learning packages such as distance learning, videos, CDs, workbooks, and textbooks.

6.15 Summing Up

6.15.1 Customer defined

The term customer is defined as follows: 'The consumer of the products and services of an organization, often called the external customer, and everyone within the organization who is in effect an "internal customer".'

6.15.2 **PACT meetings**

PACT is the name given to the neighbourhood meetings that will form the structure through which Neighbourhood Policing will be delivered. PACT stands for Partnerships And Communities Together.

6.15.3. **The functions of a meeting**

A meeting is a discussion involving two or more people and has six main functions which are shown below:

- they provide an opportunity for exchanges to take place quickly;
- they provide an environment whereby people can offer new ideas;
- they lessen some of the difficulties encountered in face-to-face meetings;
- people who attend meetings are more likely to become committed to new ideas;
- they increase teamwork and can empower individuals;
- they are used to explain why things are happening and provide an opportunity to answer questions.

6.15.4 **Minutes of a meeting**

Minutes are a record of a meeting which can be used to prompt action, identify who is responsible for what, and the timescales involved. It can also be used later on to justify action taken or show the official record of what took place at the meeting. An agenda is a list of things to be done or, in the case of meetings, items of business to be considered. In most cases this needs to be in writing and circulated well in advance.

6.15.5 **The make up of meetings**

A meeting should:

- have a purpose;
- achieve its purpose;
- take only as much time as necessary;
- involve only the people who need to be there;
- result in action, not words.

6.15.6. **Before a meeting**

One should always:

- study all the material that has been circulated before the meeting;
- start and finish on time;

- stick to the agenda at all times;
- make sure that everyone involved in the meeting is fully aware of any decisions that have been made;
- ensure, especially if you are the chairperson, that as many people as possible are involved in any question and answer session.

6.15.7 **The PDR**

This system of Performance and Development Review (PDR) is intended to be a continuous process which improves motivation, skills, and abilities and also to encourage the best possible performance from people, whatever job they are carrying out for the organization.

6.15.8. **SMARTER—mnemonic for action planning**

S	Specific	precisely worded and accurate
M	Measurable	the word 'better' cannot be measured whereas a percentage can be
A	Achievable	it needs to be within the person's ability and range
R	Relevant	to the needs of the force and wishes of the individual
T	Time constrained	setting a time when progress will be reviewed

In particular in terms of the PDR process they should also:

E	Enhance performance
R	Raise standards

References and Further Reading

Forsyth, P. (2001) *Making Meetings Work*, London: CIPD.
Hindle, T. (1998) *Managing Meetings*, London: Dorling Kindersley.
Melnico W.B. and Mennig, J.C. (2002) *Elements of Police Supervision*, London: Collier Macmillan.

Useful websites

A free website on how to run meetings available at <http://www.businessballs.com/meetings.htm>.

SPACE FOR NOTES

SPACE FOR NOTES

SPACE FOR NOTES

PART THREE

Practical Leadership

7

Communication Skills
for Leaders

7.1 **Introduction**

The police organization could not exist without communication. Staff constantly communicate with other people, the public, colleagues, those who are managers, and those we aspire to lead. We communicate by telephone, e-mail, the written word, word of mouth, and non-verbal communication (NVC), such as the way we stand or sit. Communication is vital for the police service when it comes to interacting with its customers. It must provide information to and also receive information from, the public in order to try and fulfil its many functions. This is achieved in many ways but all forces now have dedicated websites in an effort to interact with members of the public. Before reading on, try Exercise 7A below.

EXERCISE 7A   Force websites

Visit at least four different websites from police forces. Write down how they are being used, and the different kinds of information and communication methods that are contained in them.

Communication can be a complicated or a simple process, as the person who starts the communication has to make sure that the right words are chosen in order for the receiver to clearly understand what is meant.

7.2 **The Communication Process**

In terms of the communication process, as a sender, you have to choose the right words. This is known as 'encoding' the message. The person you are communicating with, the receiver, receives the message from you. Using all their previous communication experiences the receiver 'decodes' the message from you. The following illustrates this process. As a team leader you ask a member of the team why they have failed to complete a task. As a sender you have several ways of 'encoding'. This could be 'What the devil do you think you are doing?' to 'I see that the task has not been achieved. Is there any reason why this should be so?'

Once the message has been sent, you read the recipients non-verbal communications (NVCs) to obtain some kind of feedback. This could be a look of amazement or even anger. At the same time, the recipient is reading your NVCs to try and gauge how serious perhaps you are, or where is the communication between you going to lead.

The communication process also occurs within what is sometimes referred to as 'noise' or background/context. There are many factors that introduce noise into the process and can become barriers to the communication process. Figure 7.1 below illustrates the communication process.

Figure 7.1 The communication process

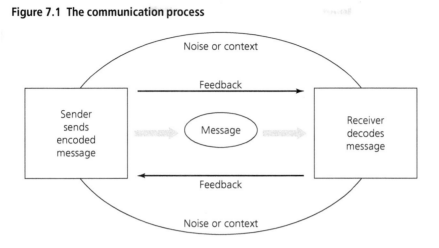

The noise or context which forms the background to the communication process is very important and highly influential. They can in fact become barriers to the communication process, and as an effective leader and communicator you will need to consider these barriers and understand where they come from.

7.2.1 **Barriers to communication**

There are in the main three types of barriers to the communication process which can lead to disruption in the transmission of messages. They are as follows:

- physical barriers
- perception barriers
- psychological barriers.

Each of these will be considered below.

Physical barriers to communication

First, try Exercise 7B below.

EXERCISE 7B Physical barriers to communication

Using your experience, and also by discussing this with others, make a list of what you consider to be physical barriers to communication.

You may have considered some of the following as physical barriers to communication:

- a room that was too cold for a meeting;
- too much background noise created by people talking;

- speaking too loudly over the phone because you are not sure of the quality of the connection;
- the environment has distractions for the people involved in the communication process.

The point to remember is that choosing the right time and place is vital if the communication process is to be effective.

Perception barriers

These barriers are caused by the different way in which we perceive those with whom we communicate. In the main, these types of barriers are caused by:

- Stereotyping so that we have preconceived ideas about how an individual may react or behave.
- A past experience, either good or bad, so that a person might pre-judge the expected response.
- Being overly influenced by rank or status.
- An emotional response which is not appropriate to the response expected.

As communicators we should be aware that these barriers caused by our perceptions exist and can dramatically influence our expected responses from individuals.

Psychological barriers

As a reflective practitioner and good communicator we need to understand that within each one of us there may exist psychological barriers that could greatly influence the communication process. Some of the common psychological barriers that exist are:

- *Denial*—this means refusing to accept that something has happened or that it has had an effect upon you. Sometimes talking with a colleague after a traumatic incident may result in them wanting to deny its effects.
- *Displacement*—this implies the idea that is the opposite of what we really feel or believe.
- *Rationalization*—this means trying to apply a logical justification for an unacceptable position or decision.
- *Projection*—this means transferring the problem or unacceptable view to someone else.

The society in which the police organization operates is becoming increasingly multicultural and diverse. Leaders in the police need to be aware of the impact cross-cultural communication can have on our ability to understand what others are trying to communicate to us. People tend to read behaviour from their own cultural group, without being aware of the possibility of different meanings attributed to it in the culture of the other person. This applies to both verbal and non-verbal communication and it is important to understand and appreciate possible cross-cultural barriers to communication.

7.3 **Becoming a More Effective Communicator**

A reflective practitioner and leader must be able to take stock of their own ability and capacity to communicate with others. Further, they must consider the communication skills within those who they work with.

EXERCISE 7C Effective communicators

Think about people you know, either in the workplace or outside, that you consider to be good communicators. Write down what you think there is about them that makes them good communicators?

Having compiled your list in the exercise above, compare them to the following which are considered essential in an individuals who can communicate effectively. These are:

- saying something more clearly;
- reflecting upon ourselves as communicators;
- becoming a better listener.

These are discussed below.

7.3.1 **Saying something more clearly**

There have probably been times when you have had a conversation with someone and you have been impatient for them to get to the point! Further, there may have been occasions when someone has missed out essential details which have required you to question them about. Sometimes we are all guilty of saying something which could have been said in a more clear and concise manner. Feedback from others regarding this should always be welcome as it will build up your confidence in your communication skills.

7.3.2 **Reflecting upon ourselves as communicators**

This can be quite difficult for an individual to achieve, but is necessary if we are to improve our communication skills. Think about those individuals at work or elsewhere that you have difficulty communicating with. It may be that your projected image of yourself may cause some of the problems you are experiencing as other may consider you unapproachable or not concerned about them. Reflecting upon ourselves can improve the communication process.

7.3.3 **Becoming a better listener**

Listening is probably the most important skill that a good communicator can have. Active listening will ensure that you can understand the intentions of the speaker when they communicate with you. Transformational leaders should engage in this approach as it shows you have a genuine interest in people, being available to them and putting their needs before yours. Having stated how important listening is try the following exercise.

EXERCISE 7D Why don't people listen?

Compile a list of the reasons why you think people do not listen properly.

You may have thought of the following:

- Lack of attention—this occurs when people withdraw their attention and focus on something else.
- Being judgemental—this occurs when by use of non-verbal signals or by interruptions; they let you know they are not interested.
- Being too busy—this occurs when the person has started a major task and wants to get on with it.
- Lack of engagement—this occurs when the person is not interested and does not listen to what is being said and gives the wrong responses.
- Being selective—this occurs when a person only listens to the parts of the conversation they want to hear and only respond to those issues.

There are several ways of improving your listening skills. These are shown in the following Key Point box.

KEY POINT—IMPROVING YOUR LISTENING SKILLS

1. Go into the conversation with an open mind.
2. Attend to the speaker and avoid distractions.
3. Avoid speaking across speakers.
4. Restate key points from time to time.
5. Paraphrase and reflect on your understanding.
6. Give feedback and other responses as appropriate.
7. Allow for reflection by using attentive silence and spaces in the conversation.

Feedback

A key skill in the communication process is to give and receive constructive feedback. Doing this positively and effectively in a leadership role calls for very distinct skills. Before reading on, consider the following exercise.

EXERCISE 7E Feedback

Consider the following:

1. A colleague in your workplace informs you that you are constantly making the same mistake and that you should address the issue.
2. A family member tells you that you are always leaving unwashed dishes lying around and that you should wash them after use.

Would you react differently to these two feedback scenarios, which in effect are the same? Try to think why this should be the case.

We all react differently to critical comments. Sometimes it is easier to accept them from friends or family, whereas the same type of views from colleagues and others may trigger off a defensive reaction. Whenever you have the opportunity to give or receive feedback, then the following may be useful. Feedback needs to be:

- objective and not judgemental;
- specific and supported by observed behaviour;
- relevant to the person being helped;
- as soon after the event as possible.

Feedback is most effective when people ask for it, rather than when it is offered to them without their asking for it. Feedback will be wasted if it is offered in such a way that the colleague resists hearing or using what is offered, or if they are not prepared to hear it or use it for a whole host of reasons.

7.4 Counselling and Counselling Skills in the Workplace

As a police leader you will on occasions find yourself dealing with issues that require counselling skills. Occasionally, you will identify a situation that is beyond your skills and abilities to deal with and you will then need to ensure that qualified help is available for the work colleague. If the problem is of a serious operational or personal nature then people may have to withdraw from their normal role whilst professional assessments and help can be provided.

It may be that someone has been exposed to traumatic incidents, or have been subject to harassment or victimization. Occasionally, someone who you work with needs to help because their work performance has deteriorated dramatically because of a personal problem. The more others come to regard you as a leader, the more likely you will find yourself having to deal with this kind of situation. As a leader, however, you are not automatically a qualified counsellor. You would not necessarily have the qualifications to deal with, for example, individuals who suffer from post traumatic stress syndrome. However, if you are able to offer support and understanding as a front line response to help staff this is very beneficial. The ability to use counselling skills and the ability to identify when someone needs professional counselling in a working relationship is therefore very important. Now try exercise 7F.

EXERCISE 7F Professional counselling

What symptoms or behaviour would you expect to see in a colleague who might need professional counselling?

As a leader you may have considered some of the following:

- physical symptoms;
- changes in behaviour, moodiness, and relationship problems;
- unusual or extreme symptoms such as depression or fears.

These signs and symptoms must be brought to the attention of professional counselling and medical staff as soon as possible. You will need to explain to the individual that you do not feel able to provide the type of support they need but will continue to support them as best you can.

7.4.1 Using counselling skills

One of the main points about using counselling skills in the workplace is that ownership of the particular problem has to remain with the individual concerned, as well as the goals, the plans and the resulting changes they choose to make. Without this, counselling will not occur or be successful.

There are six stages to using counselling skills in the workplace. These are as follows:

1. building a helping relationship;
2. helping the person understand the problem;
3. helping them set goals;
4. helping them plan and take action;
5. consolidating the change;
6. withdrawal.

Each of these stages will be briefly considered below.

Building a relationship

After deciding whether or not you are the best person to be offering the help, you will need to ensure that you agree ground rules about issues such as confidentiality as well as what exactly you are prepared to do to help. This must be discussed and agreed between you and the individual concerned before proceeding on to the second phase of utilizing counselling skills.

Helping them understand the problem

During this stage, you will help the individual recognize what the problem is and then encourage them to think about possible solutions to the problem. It is here that you will need to use very good listening communication skills, as well as encouraging the individual to recognize the fact that they need to act.

Helping them set goals

At this stage, you will start to employ your leadership skills in the area of problem-solving. The individual concerned should be encouraged to consider a range of alternatives and then choose which goal to pursue. Sometimes the individual will fixate upon one solution, so you will need to ensure that alternatives are considered.

At this point try Exercise 7G below.

EXERCISE 7G Techniques to prevent fixation on one solution

Consider some techniques that will ensure an individual does not fixate on one solution without exploring as widely as possible. Write down some of your ideas.

You may have thought of conducting a mind mapping exercise or board blasting as a way of breaking out of a fixation on one solution.

Helping them plan and take action

At this stage, you and the individual should discuss the means of achieving the agreed goal. You should encourage the individual to consider as widely as possible, whilst being realistic, to improve their chances of success.

Consolidating the change

This is a vital area in the whole process. People very often make resolutions only to rescind on them shortly afterwards. One way of ensuring this does not happen is to introduce some form of monitoring through feedback sessions from the person whom you are helping.

Withdrawal

As a leader engaged in using your counselling skills, you are not concerned with a long-term helping arrangement as this would indicate that you have failed to help them with their problem. The best feedback you can have is when the individual whom you have been helping believes that they have achieved the solution by themselves.

7.4.2 **Counselling qualities**

As a leader you must be aware of the qualities that you should possess to enable you to engage effectively with colleagues in the counselling process. The qualities that are essentially required of a transformational leader are:

- Being self-aware—this means being aware of your own norms and values and your experiences which have helped shape your views.
- Being yourself—this means being aware of your own feelings and trying to be transparent and real as you listen and support the other person. People are likely to see through a persona you project that is not really you.
- Being empathetic—This means listening and being sensitive and clarifying what you have heard being said to you. You need to be understanding of the other person, to communicate this understanding and evaluate what you are being told without being judgemental.
- Being accepting of people—this means taking people as they are.

Remember, in order for you to help other people they must trust you and experience a non-judgemental welcome from you.

7.5 **Assertiveness and Communication**

As a leader you need to be direct, unambiguous, and fair when dealing with others and also achieving your goals and directing a situation. Straightness and fairness tend to gain respect from those that we lead. Being assertive can on occasions be misunderstood, as an easy option is to raise your voice to get your point across. However, when properly used, assertiveness is a harder approach than a display of anger, as it requires you to be very sure of your ground and often needs moral courage in the face of determined and sometimes aggressive individuals. First, we need to consider just what we mean by assertiveness. Try the following exercise before moving on.

EXERCISE 7H Assertiveness

Write down what you think is meant by being assertive.
What type of outcome do you think an assertive person is hoping to achieve?

Assertiveness is behaviour where you make clear your rights whilst respecting the rights of others. The type of outcome an assertive person hopes to achieve is a win-win outcome or a solution where both parties gain something. This involves an element of compromise from both parties to ensure that the advantage does not rest just with one individual.

KEY POINT—ASSERTIVENESS

Assertiveness is behaviour where you make clear your rights whilst respecting the rights of others. The type of outcome an assertive person hopes to achieve is a win-win outcome or a solution where both parties gain something.

Assertiveness is just one form of behaviour that people engage in when dealing with others. There is in the main three other types of behaviour that individual's exhibit. These are:

- aggression—or behaviour where one claims their rights at the expense of other people's rights. This results in a win-lose situation, the aggressor being the apparent winner;
- compliance—or behaviour where people choose to accept the other person's views when faced with aggression. This is considered a lose-win encounter where one concedes one's rights to pacify the aggressor.
- manipulation—this is the least productive type of engagement where neither party assert their rights and the end result is a lose-lose situation.

Having considered the four types of behaviour discussed above, it may be assumed that assertiveness is the best type of encounter as we all prefer a win-win exchange. That said, it is sometimes difficult to realize this sort of outcome, which requires much skill on the part of the leader. Try the following exercise in order to appreciate the advantages and disadvantages of the four behaviour types discussed above. In each box, one answer has already been provided for you. Try to add at least two more.

EXERCISE 7I Advantages and disadvantages of behaviour

Behaviour	Advantages	Disadvantages
Aggressive	Short-term compliance.	People resent you.
Compliant	You have a peaceful time.	People will take advantage of you.
Manipulative	You feel superior.	You will lose other people's respect for you.
Assertive	People understand clearly what you want.	You risk confrontation.

Once you have completed this exercise you will see that there are choices to be made when you interact with people especially in the role of a leader. You cannot change your personality, but you can inform and change your attitudes and behaviour in a way that will help other people.

7.5.1 **Developing self-assertiveness**

Before you can begin behaving assertively, you need to think assertively. Learning to think assertively is a good foundation for later on. To help in this process, there are two main areas that need examining. These are:

- the way you talk to yourself; and
- your rights.

The two areas are discussed below.

Talking to yourself

This means the little conversations you have with yourself that situate your feelings that you associate with a given situation. This occurs within your sub-conscious and sometimes we do not realize we are actually having these conversations. These conversations are also known as inner dialogues and occur at a much faster rate than normal speech conversations. Talking to yourself is important because:

- it is the earliest point in the interaction process at which you can intervene and make it work to your advantage;
- intervening in the process requires conscious thought which means that you can turn negative feelings into positive ones;
- working with 'words' is easier than working with emotions.

The following example in Table 7.1 illustrates this process.

Table 7.1 Using self-talk

	Before self-talk	After self-talk
Situation	Senior officer, with raised voice, points at you and asks you why you aren't doing your job properly.	Same.
Self-talk	'This is not fair, the boss is always picking on me, I am useless.'	The approach used is not nice, but by listening I can try to find out why the boss is being like this. The boss is not criticizing me as a person.
Feelings	Feelings of inadequacy, loss of power, low self-esteem.	Concern that the senior officer may have misunderstood something and not have a clear picture of things.
Behaviour	Passive and accepting, defensive answers.	Assertive. Listening. Acknowledging concerns and helping get the facts straight.
Outcome	Boss's view apparently reinforced, leading to lack of respect from boss.	Boss's view corrected, ground rules established for future interactions, inspires self-esteem.

The idea is that it is possible to control situations and can actually intervene beneath the surface of events to make it work for you rather than against you. After considering the above, try Exercise 7J.

EXERCISE 7J Self-talk

Think of an example where you have behaved passively in an interaction with others and construct your own table like the example already shown. By doing this exercise you will realize how even small changes can influence you towards a different outcome.

You will probably notice that it can be difficult knowing what your self-talk is as these inner dialogues occur at a fast rate of speed. However, with practice you will find that you can control your inner responses to situations that will lead to a more positive and assertive outcome for yourself.

Your rights

A right is something to which you are entitled. There are no preconditions attached to rights and you do not have to justify them in any way. In England and Wales, for example, there are laws to protect an individual in the workplace from discrimination, to provide health and safety, and to protect an individual from harassment. These are fairly easy to identify, but there are some that are not included in Acts of Parliament, but relate to how we interact with each other. As an individual you have the general right to the following:

- to be treated with respect;
- to state what you want or how you feel;
- to have and express an opinion;
- to be listened to;
- to make mistakes like everyone else.

Appreciating your general rights will help your understanding of interactions and assist in being more assertive. However, when thinking about your rights, it is all too easy to just consider your own in your favour. Other people have rights as well, and rights also carry responsibilities. For example, if you insist on the right to be listened to, then you have the responsibility to listen to others. To help understand this viewpoint try the following exercise.

EXERCISE 7K The concept of rights

Think of at least two situations where you behaved passively and aggressively with another person. Write down what you thought were your rights in each occasion. Now write down what you think may have been the other person's rights. By doing so, you can reflect upon the outcomes of the situations and how they may have been altered.

7.6 **Presentations**

Leaders within the police service are called upon to deliver presentations for many and varied audiences. This may be presentations to senior officers about the crime statistics for their areas, internal briefing for staff about to embark on a police operation, or even members of the public about police strategy within their neighbour partnership area. It is therefore vital that some knowledge about how to prepare and deliver presentations as a communication tool is known by the police leader.

7.6.1 **Benefits of giving presentations**

There are several good reasons for giving presentations as a form of communication. These are:

- time critical information can be communicated to a large group of people;
- the need to persuade an audience to change its mind;
- the audience are interested and want to hear what you have to say;
- it is more cost effective to communicate the information to a large group rather than one or two people;
- there are a clear set of objectives for the purpose of the presentation.

There are several important phases to giving a good presentation. These include:

- considering the subject of the presentation;
- considering the audience you are presenting to;
- writing your script;
- rehearsal;
- delivering the presentation;
- handling question and answer session.

These important areas will now be considered in more detail.

7.6.2 **The subject of the presentation.**

Generally speaking, whenever you give a presentation it is fair to say you will already know the subject you are going to present. Usually this has been defined by yourself or another person who wants you to deliver the presentation on their behalf. Whilst this may seem straightforward, there remains the problem of just what you need to tell the audience and how much information you need to impart to them. Any presentation, no matter how simple or straightforward it first appears, can be delivered in many different ways in terms of content. For example, if you are delivering a presentation on crime and disorder statistics in a particular area, are you just going to give the facts straight, or are you going to engage in some form of interpretation and explanation of the figures? However, for any presentation to be effective, it must be delivered effectively and must engage positively with the listeners. Consider the above and try the following exercise.

EXERCISE 7L Delivering presentations

You have been asked to deliver a presentation about the introduction of neighbourhood policing teams. What sort of presentation would you deliver to the following different groups?

1. Staff who are going to make up the teams.
2. Staff who are going to perform a support function such as Scenes of Crime officers.
3. Members of the public who will be the customers of the new teams.

Even though the basic facts are the same, you will probably use a different approach for each type of person named in the exercise above. In general, the needs of an audience for presentations include the following:

- straightforward information such as figures, results etc.;
- historical background to increase understanding of present situation;
- comparisons between different approaches/perspectives;
- interpretations of what different facts mean to different people;
- motivation to take a decision or actions;
- education so that something will be done better;
- entertainment.

Bearing in mind the list shown above, you may have considered that the information required for the groups in Exercise 7L would be as follows:

Group	Information in presentation
Staff making up teams	History and reasons for introduction, comparison to other policing methods, motivation for new methods.
Staff supporting teams	Information about new method of policing, education regarding role and aims and objectives of new policing methods.
Customers of teams	Motivation to take part, interpretation of information, and information regarding aims, objectives, and contacts.

7.6.3 **The audience you are presenting to**

This is another often neglected area of presentational work. You need to know about your audience before you start to prepare your presentation. There are four areas that you should consider. These are:

- The audience's objectives—these are often tied to their role they play, for example their part in the neighbourhood team. They may need to know what

165

they are to do with the information from the presentation, or they may only be interested in a part of the presentation.

- The audience's knowledge—the presenter must always consider the level of knowledge that the audience possesses. For example, using police terminology such as jargon or acronyms, for a presentation to members of the public could be confusing. Further, the background of the audience may mean that they have a thorough knowledge of the subject you are presenting about, so you may need to consider why they are there. They may be expecting a different interpretation of existing knowledge, which will influence your presentation.
- Previous contact between you and your audience—There may be a history between you and your audience or at least parts of the audience. This is important as you may well find much support for your presentation from them. Alternatively, they may be disruptive and cast doubt on your presentation and your interpretation of facts. This is an area that is easy to overlook but can play a big part in the success or otherwise of your presentation.
- Audience information assimilation—We all have different preferences as to the way in which we take on board information. Presenters have their own style of delivery, based on the way we as individuals behave, and individuals in audiences also have preferences for certain ways of receiving and assimilating information. For example, if you are giving a presentation on crime and disorder to senior police officers, they may want you to concentrate on facts and figures, including trends and costs of staff involvement, delivered in formal manner, in order to satisfy performance targets. The same presentation to members of a community in a public meeting may not be so concerned about these facts and figures, but may want more information about high visibility patrolling delivered in a more relaxed manner.

Once you have researched your audience and decided exactly what they want and what you want out of your presentation, you need to consider writing a script that underpins your talk.

7.6.4 Writing your script

People who regularly deliver successful presentations have a system of writing their scripts, so the lesson is once you have found a system that works for you, stay with it!

For those who are starting out the following will be useful:

- Once you have decided the subject and purpose of the presentation collect all the information that will make up the bulk of the presentation.
- Write down the points one by one on a separate small sheet of paper.
- Try using just single key words at this stage, as all you need at this stage is to get your ideas into a logical and prioritized manner.
- Experiment with the order in which you intend to make your points.

- Once you have these in a logical order/group decide which require examples to make them clear and which may need additional visual aids to help get over your point.
- Decide how you intend to link the groups of information together so that they appear seamless.

Even if using IT as the basis for the delivery of your presentation, it is useful to write down your presentation just in case the technology fails. Some people like to write out the whole presentation and then condense it onto small cards, whilst others like to write down bullet points and make brief notes to remind them of the examples/evidence they are going to use. Remember though that reading verbatim from a script sounds artificial and may well undermine your presentation and your credibility. Cue cards should be used as an aid to your presentation, something to keep you on track and ensure that you discuss all the points you need to.

Once you have worked through this process, you need to divide your presentation into three main stages. These are:

- The Introduction—this section sets the scene, catches the audience's attention, establishes the expectations of the presentation, and engages the listener. A good presenter will have thought out a title for the presentation, and can engage the audience positively at this point. For example, if you are delivering a presentation on consultation with the community to members of the local Crime and Disorder Reduction Partnership, you could use the title *Section 17 of the Crime and Disorder Act 1998* which underpins the consultation process for partnership policing. However, a sub-title such as *'Its good to talk!'* says much more and sets the expectations of a presentation that is tailored to the real needs of the audience.
- The Main Body—This is where the presenter fleshes out the main points of the presentation. Examples of what has been talked about are given here, as well as references to support your points and help convince the audience of the truth of what you are saying. However, do not go into so much detail that you overwhelm your audience but it is useful to remember that an audience will remember most points if they are displayed visually. This does not mean, however, that you can overdose your audience on visual displays, but use slides to support what you are saying through charts, photographs, cartoons and other types of graphics.
- The Ending—A strong ending to your presentation will leave a good impression and supports all the good work you have done. Conversely, a weak ending can undo all your hard work in the first two parts of the presentation. In this section, the presenter will need to summarize the points considered in the main body of the presentation, and should be clear and concise summary, not merely a reiteration of the main section. Once this has been achieved, you can then ask the audience to become involved by requesting any questions etc. Finally, you need to ensure that your contact details are available should anyone have a question on your presentation in future.

Visual aids are useful in any presentation, not only to prompt the presenter but also to ensure that the audience understands the points covered. There are a wide variety of visual aids available to the presenter and these are considered in Table 7.2 below.

Table 7.2 Visual aids

Visual Aid	Comments
Flip charts	Writing needs to be big and clear enough to be seen from the back of the audience.
Overhead projector	Check that it is in working order before presentation starts. Position in such a manner that it does not block the view of the audience. Ensure that the information is situated in the centre of the slide and that it is written in a font large enough to be seen.
IT software	Easy to use and visually attractive with many extras attached such as sound. Always have a backup as occasionally the software may not function correctly.
Handouts	Most audiences will contain people who will want some sort of backup material. Make sure this are available *after* your presentation otherwise people will read it and not pay attention to your presentation.

7.6.5 **Rehearsal**

Being prepared to deliver your presentation means that you have to work through the rehearsal process. In a sense it is like giving evidence in court, in that one prepares oneself by going over the evidence that is to be delivered and anticipating any areas that will stimulate questions. Read through your presentation and memorize the structure and main points of your presentation. Also, it is useful to get a friend to listen and see your presentation as a rehearsal, as they may point out obvious problems that you may have missed, such as the misspelling of words on a presentation slide, or the fact that you tend to talk to fast. If you are using IT software then it pays to rehearse with it to ensure it works correctly. Remember, the more important the presentation, the more rehearsal is needed.

Rehearsing your presentation is important because:

- it allows you to experiment with the actual words that you are going to use;
- it allows you to work out the actual timing of the presentation;
- it acts as a quality assurance on your cue cards, IT, or other presentation aids;
- it allows constructive feedback from a 'friendly' audience;
- it helps you to learn and understand the presentation.

Once you have rehearsed your presentation and adjusted it through the feedback you have received you will be far more confident in its delivery.

7.6.6 **Delivering the presentation**

Your initial entrance when giving your presentation is very important. An important point to remember is not to appear too rushed as this will immediately impact upon the perception the audience will have about you. Take a slow deep breath and try to relax as you ensure that everything you need for the presentation is with you. Check that any IT or flipcharts are in order and when you are satisfied take up your position and look at the audience. It is important to be pleasant so do not be afraid to smile at the audience and begin confidently by saying 'good morning/afternoon/evening' and introducing yourself. Once you begin your presentation, remember that there are several problem areas that you will want to avoid. These are:

- don't speak too quietly or too quickly;
- don't avoid eye contact with the audience;
- don't bend or twist your body, it is important to stand straight although there is no problem with moving around as you present your work;
- don't put your hands in your pockets or place them behind your back.

Although there is a list of things that you should not do whilst delivering your presentation, there are also some things you need to ensure you actually do. These are:

- when you introduce a new area/topic make sure you pause in your delivery;
- when you make an important point, make sure you slow down and raise your voice slightly;
- watch the audience closely as they will give you clues as to how the presentation is being received.

As you reach the end of your presentation it is tempting to speed up your delivery in order to get it over with. Make an extra effort to slow down a little and actually raise the level of your voice to ensure that you have the audience's attention as you finish your presentation. At the end of every successful presentation there should be a question and answer session, and this is discussed below.

7.6.7 **Handling question and answer sessions**

This gives the audience the opportunity to speak following your presentation. Many people dread this part of the process as they fear they suffer criticism from a hostile audience. In reality this occurs on very few occasions. However, although this is true, this does not mean the presenter can relax. A well-handled question and answer session has several benefits including the following:

- answers seem more credible as the presenter is not working from their script;
- the audience has a chance to gain greater insights into the parts of the presentation that affects them;

- the questions will give you the opportunity to reinforce the main points of your presentation.

Sometimes you may get an individual who, because perhaps of their personal agenda, wants to air their grievances. This can in some respects be controlled by placing constraints at the beginning of the question and answer session such as:

- placing a time limit on the session itself;
- limiting the number of people allowed to ask questions;
- taking written questions only;
- using the facilitator or person in charge to decide which questions will be dealt with.

Broadly speaking, questions can be placed into particular categories and this allows us to consider particular responses to them. Table 7.3 illustrates the types of questions you could face and how you should respond to them.

Table 7.3 Types of questions and responses

Question type	How to respond
Clearing up (more information required)	These questions should always be answered as they give you a chance to reinforce what you have already said.
Detailed (how many/how much?)	Answer these if you can, but keep your responses brief as you know the audience will probably be interested.
Rambling ('I remember when . . .')	Once they have made their point, offer your thanks and then turn to the audience and ask for further questions.
Next time (Will you be discussing?)	If you are going to cover the points in future, answer giving the audience a taster of things to come so that they will be interested in attending the next presentation!
Explosive (I have been researching what you say about . . .)	Try not to answer these and state that such matters are outside the remit of the presentation or that this is not the appropriate time to discuss the points.

Whatever question is directed at you, it is important to listen all the way through it as sometimes we can stop listening halfway through. This means that the answer supplied is often based only on the first part of the question.

Once you have listened to the question there is a technique that you may find useful in answering it. This is called the DRAT method. DRAT stands for:

D Decide if you are going to answer the question.
R Rephrase or repeat the question so that the audience hears it.
A Answer the question briefly and clearly.
T Thank the person asking the question.

Using this framework gives one the feeling of control and so if anything difficult should occur this technique will help handle it.

7.6.8 Closing the presentation

Once the question and answer session is completed, then you need to draw the presentation to a close. Again you need to consider taking time over this phase of the presentation. Here you can:

- summarize your main points again; and
- remind the audience of any outcomes from the presentation.

These should be kept brief but use emphasis and enthusiasm to put them across. Leave your audience in a positive frame of mind finishing your presentation by thanking everyone for their attention.

7.7 Report Writing

A report may be defined as a formal statement of the results of an investigation, of any matter on which definite information is required, made by some person, or body instructed or required to do so. They are written to record, inform, and to recommend and are regularly used by the police service to convey information about specific matters.

A report serves two main purposes:

- It provides a permanent, comprehensive, and coherent account of an investigation, study, or piece of research.
- It provides information, which is required for decision-making.

By perfecting the art of report writing you will be improving your performance not only as a leader, but also as a researcher or investigator.

7.7.1 The structure of the report

Rules are required to ensure all reports comply with the same corporate approach. This also assists everyone because of the use of a common style. The contents of a report should include the following main headings:

Title—includes the title, subtitle, the writer(s) of the report, the recipient of the report, the date of the report.

Summary or abstract—Normally one paragraph (50 to 100 words) or one page (300 to 400 words). It is a précis of the whole report (see example below).

List of contents—a list of chapters or sections as they appear in the report, giving the page on which it begins.

Introduction—This will include the events leading up to the request for the report, terms of reference, resources available to the writer, or acknowledgment of help from others.

Body of report under headings—(see section below on headings).

A conclusion—Here the author looks back upon the work and delivers the verdict. It may involve comparing different possibilities and it is here that the report may look more like an essay.

Recommendations—Recommendations should be kept short, crisp, and to the point avoiding overlaps with the conclusion.

Appendices—This may include a list of sources or a bibliography. It may also contain tables or diagrams, and sometimes in technical reports a glossary of terms used in the report.

7.7.2 Headings used in the body of the report

Some form of numbering in the main body of the report is essential for ease of reference. One of the most common forms is that called the *Decimal Notation System*. In this system, main sections within the body of the report are given single numbers (1, 2, 3 etc.) in numerical order. The first level of subsection under the major section will follow a decimal point (1.1) and the first subsection under that subsection will repeat the process. Usually three levels of numbering are sufficient. For example, if we were to organize a report on crime prevention, then the contents may be organized as shown in the following key point box.

KEY POINT—THE STRUCTURE OF A REPORT

3. Crime Prevention (*the main section heading*)

3.1 Burglary (*the 1st subsection heading*)
3.1.1 Windows (*1st subsection under 1st subsection*)
3.1.2 Doors. (*2nd subsection under 1st subsection*)
3.1.3 Property (*3rd subsection under 1st subsection*)

3.2 Auto-crime (*the 2nd subsection heading*)
3.2.1 Theft of vehicles (*2nd subsection under 2nd subsection*)
3.2.2 Theft from vehicles (*2nd subsection under 1st subsection*)

3.3 Violent crime (*the 3rd subsection heading*)
3.3.1 Robbery (*1st subsection under 2nd subsection*)
3.3.2 Grievous Bodily Harm (*2nd subsection under 1st subsection*)

7.8 **Summing Up**

7.8.1 **Barriers to communication**

There are, in the main, three types of barriers to the communication process which can lead to disruption in the transmission of messages. They are as follows:

- physical barriers;
- perception barriers;
- psychological barriers.

7.8.2 **Improving Listening skills**

You can improve your listening skills by:

- Going into the conversation with an open mind.
- Attending to the speaker and avoiding distractions.
- Avoiding speaking across speakers.
- Restating key points from time to time.
- Paraphrasing and reflecting on your understanding.
- Giving feedback and other responses as appropriate.
- Allowing for reflection by using attentive silence and spaces in the conversation.

7.8.3 **Feedback**

Feedback needs to be:

- objective and not judgemental;
- specific and supported by observed behaviour;
- relevant to the person being helped;
- as soon after the event as possible.

7.8.4 **Stages of using counselling skills**

There are six stages to using counselling skills in the workplace. These are as follows:

1. building a helping relationship;
2. helping the person understand the problem;
3. helping them set goals;
4. helping them plan and take action;
5. consolidating the change;
6. withdrawal.

Qualities required of a transformational leader engaged in counselling

These qualities are essentially:

- being self-aware—this means being aware of your own norms and values and your experiences which have helped shape your views.
- being yourself—this means being aware of your own feelings and trying to be transparent and real as you listen and support the other person. People are likely to see through a persona you project that is not really you.
- being empathetic—This means listening and being sensitive and clarifying what you have heard being said to you. You need to be understanding of the other person, to communicate this understanding, and evaluate what you are being told without being judgemental.
- being accepting of people—this means taking people as they are.

7.8.5 Assertiveness

Assertiveness is behaviour where you make clear your rights whilst respecting the rights of others. The type of outcome an assertive person hopes to achieve is a win-win outcome or a solution where both parties gain something.

Thinking assertively

Learning to think assertively is a good foundation. To help in this process, there are two main areas that need examining. These are:

- the way you talk to yourself and;
- your rights.

7.8.6 Reasons supporting the use of presentations

There are several good reasons for giving presentations as a form of communication. These are:

- time-critical information can be communicated to a large group of people;
- the need to persuade an audience to change its mind;
- the audience are interested and want to hear what you have to say;
- it is more cost effective to communicate the information to a large group rather than one or two people;
- there are a clear set of objectives for the purpose of the presentation.

Technique for answering questions

Once you have listened to a question there is a technique that you may find useful in answering it. This is called the DRAT method.

7.8.7 **Definition of a report**

A report may be defined as a formal statement of the results of an investigation, of any matter on which definite information is required, made by some person, or body instructed or required to do so.

Why use reports?

A report serves two main purposes:

- It provides a permanent, comprehensive, and coherent account of an investigation, study, or piece of research.
- It provides information, which is required for decision-making.

References and Further Reading

Fast, J. (1997) *Body Language: The Essential Secrets of Non-Verbal Communication*, London: MJF Books.

Gillen, T. (2003) *Assertiveness*, Trowbridge: The Cromwell Press.

Hayes, J. (1996) *Developing the Manager as a Helper*, London: Routledge.

McLeod, J. (2003) *An Introduction to Counselling*, Open University Press.

Roma, K. and Raphaelson, J. (2000) *Writing That Works*, London: Harper-Collins Publications.

Siddons, S. (2003) *Presentation Skills*, Trowbridge: The Cromwell Press.

Townsend, A. (1991) *Developing Assertiveness*, London: Routledge.

Useful websites

The National Policing Improvement Agency available at <http://www.npia. police.uk/>.

A free website dedicated to personal development available at <http://www. selfgrowth.com/comm.html>.

A website looking at all aspects of interpersonal communications available at <http://www.communicationandconflict.com/interpersonal-communication. html>.

A website showing how to improve writing skills available at <http://www. selfgrowth.com/writing.html>.

SPACE FOR NOTES

SPACE FOR NOTES

SPACE FOR NOTES

Motivating Staff

> Motivation is the art of getting people to do what you want them to do
> because they want to do it.
>
> (Dwight D. Eisenhower, former President of the USA)

8.1 Introduction

Motivating people is one of the leader's main roles. Because people are different
and complex, then motivation can also be complex. Mullins (1996) tried to simplify the idea of motivation by highlighting its relationship with performance in
the workplace. For Mullins the relationship was as follows:

$$\text{Performance in work} = \text{Individual Ability} \times \text{Motivation}$$

For example, someone who is new to a team and is ambitious and is keen, but
has no or little experience will not provide the best performance. Similarly, an
experienced member of staff who is a competent worker, but has no motivation
will not give an effective performance.

The way that a leader motivates others depends upon their own assumptions
and understanding of them. Different people are motivated by different things,
so there will be a wide number of motivators at work for every different person
at whatever level in the organization they work. Motivators can be classified into
two areas, being either extrinsic or seen from the outside by others or intrinsic
or belonging to someone as basic and essential. Table 8.1 below illustrates these
motivators.

Table 8.1. Examples of motivators

Extrinsic Motivator	Intrinsic Motivator
Friendly environment	A sense of challenge
Good money	A feeling of power
Status	A sense of belonging to a group
Good annual leave conditions	Fulfilment

Having considered the different types of motivators, try Exercise 8A below.

EXERCISE 8A

Reflect upon your own motivation for the work you do and compile a list of motivators. Divide them into extrinsic and intrinsic motivators. Are there more in one
category than the other? Why do you think this might be?

8.2 **Defining Motivation**

Many authors have also defined the concept of motivation. Motivation has been defined as the psychological process that gives behaviour purpose and direction (Kreitner, 1995); a predisposition to behave in a purposeful manner to achieve specific, unmet needs (Buford and Lindner, 2001); an internal drive to satisfy an unsatisfied need and the will to achieve (Bedeian, 1993). For our purposes, motivation can be operationally defined as the inner force that drives individuals to accomplish personal and organizational goals.

KEY POINT—A WORKING DEFINITION OF MOTIVATION

The inner force that drives individuals to accomplish personal and organizational goals.

Why is there a need for a motivated workforce? The answer, perhaps, is survival. In particular there are three main areas why staff need to be motivated. These are:

• Motivated employees are needed in our rapidly changing workplaces.
• Motivated employees help organizations survive.
• Motivated employees are more productive.

To be effective, leaders need to understand what motivates staff within the context of the roles they perform. Of all the functions a leader performs, motivating staff is probably the most complex. This is due, in part, to the fact that what appears to motivate people changes constantly. For example, research suggests that as employees' income increases, money becomes less of a motivator (Kovach, 1987). Also, as a staff member get older, interesting work becomes more of a motivator.

8.3 **Motivational Theories**

Motivation is sometimes a difficult concept to understand. Why, for example, may status be a motivator for one person but not another? Further, how and why are people motivated? Mullins (1996) introduced us to another definition of motivation. He defined motivation as the driving force that causes individuals to:

• achieve specific goals;
• fulfil needs or expectations;
• uphold values.

However, there is more to motivation than this simple definition implies.

There are several important theories that attempt to provide answers to these questions and provide a framework of understanding for the leader trying to motivate individuals.

8.3.1 Maslow's hierarchy of needs

Abraham Maslow developed a theory of personality that has influenced a number of different fields, including education. This wide influence is due in part to the high level of practicality of Maslow's theory. This theory accurately describes many realities of personal experiences and many people find they can understand what Maslow says. They can recognize some features of their experience or behaviour which is true and identifiable but which they have never been able to put into words.

Maslow's approach is that of a humanistic psychologist. Humanists do not believe that human beings are pushed and pulled by mechanical forces, either of stimuli and reinforcements (behaviourism) or of unconscious instinctual impulses (psychoanalysis). Humanists focus upon potentials and they believe that humans strive for an upper level of capabilities. Humans seek the frontiers of creativity, the highest reaches of consciousness and wisdom. This has been labelled 'fully functioning person', 'healthy personality', or as Maslow calls this level, 'self-actualizing person'.

Maslow has set up a hierarchic theory of needs. All of his basic needs are basic instincts, equivalent of instincts in animals. Humans start with a very weak disposition that is then fashioned fully as the person grows. If the environment is right, people will grow straight and beautiful, actualizing the potentials they have inherited. If the environment is not 'right' (and mostly it is not) they will not grow tall and straight and beautiful.

Maslow has set up a hierarchy of five levels of basic needs. Beyond these needs, higher levels of needs exist. These include needs for understanding, aesthetical appreciation, and purely spiritual needs. In the levels of the five basic needs, the person does not feel the second need until the demands of the first have been satisfied or the third until the second has been satisfied, and so on. Maslow's basic needs are as follows:

Physiological needs

These are biological needs. They consist of needs for oxygen, food, water, and a relatively constant body temperature. They are the strongest needs because if a person were deprived of all needs, the physiological ones would come first in the person's search for satisfaction.

Safety needs

When all physiological needs are satisfied and are no longer controlling thoughts and behaviours, the needs for security can become active. Adults have little awareness of their security needs except in times of emergency or periods of dis-organization in the social structure (such as widespread rioting). Children often display the signs of insecurity and the need to be safe.

Needs for love, affection, and belongingness

When the needs for safety and for physiological well-being are satisfied, the next class of needs for love, affection, and belongingness can emerge. Maslow states that people seek to overcome feelings of loneliness and alienation. This involves both giving and receiving love, affection, and the sense of belonging.

Needs for esteem

When the first three classes of needs are satisfied, the needs for esteem can become dominant. These involve needs for both self-esteem and for the esteem a person gets from others. Humans have a need for a stable, firmly based, high level of self-respect, and respect from others. When these needs are satisfied, the person feels self-confident and valuable as a person in the world. When these needs are frustrated, the person feels inferior, weak, helpless, and worthless.

Needs for self-actualization

When all of the foregoing needs are satisfied, then and only then are the needs for self-actualization activated. Maslow describes self-actualization as a person's need to be and do that which the person was 'born to do'. For example, a musician must make music, an artist must paint, and a poet must write. These needs make themselves felt in signs of restlessness and the person feels on edge, tense, lacking something, in short, restless. If a person is hungry, unsafe, not loved or accepted, or lacking self-esteem, it is very easy to know what the person is restless about. It is not always clear what a person wants when there is a need for self-actualization. Table 8.2 below illustrates these points.

Table 8.2 Self-actualization table

Category	Need	Examples in workplace
Physiological	Food, heating and shelter	Salary, heating
Safety	Protection from danger	Job security
Social	Friendship, belonging	Good working relationships with colleagues
Self-esteem	Status and reputation	Praise and recognition
Self-actualisation	Fulfilling potential and continued development	Ability recognized and utilized to the full

The hierarchic theory is often represented as a pyramid, with the larger, lower levels representing the lower needs, and the upper point representing the need for self-actualization. This is illustrated in Figure 8.1 below.

Figure 8.1 Maslow's hierarchy of needs

Maslow believed that the only reason that people would not move well in the direction of self-actualization is because of hindrances placed in their way by society. He states that education is one of these hindrances. He recommends ways education can switch from its usual person-stunting tactics to person-growing approaches. Maslow states that educators should respond to the potential an individual has for growing into a self-actualizing person of his/her own kind. Ten points that educators should address are listed:

1. We should teach people to be *authentic*, to be aware of their inner selves and to hear their inner-feeling voices.
2. We should teach people to *transcend their cultural conditioning* and become world citizens.
3. We should help people *discover their vocation in life*, their calling, fate or destiny. This is especially focused on finding the right career and the right mate.
4. We should teach people that *life is precious*, that there is joy to be experienced in life, and if people are open to seeing the good and joyous in all kinds of situations, it makes life worth living.

5. We must *accept the person* as he or she is and helps the person learn their inner nature. From real knowledge of aptitudes and limitations we can know what to build upon, what potentials are really there?
6. We must see that the person's *basic needs are satisfied*. This includes safety, belongingness, and esteem needs.
7. We should *refresh consciousness*, teaching the person to appreciate beauty and the other good things in nature and in living.
8. We should teach people that *controls are good*, and complete abandon is bad. It takes control to improve the quality of life in all areas.
9. We should teach people to transcend the trifling problems and *grapple with the serious problems in life*. These include the problems of injustice, of pain, suffering, and death.
10. We must teach people to be *good choosers*. They must be given practice in making decisions.

Before moving on to consider a different approach, try the following exercise.

EXERCISE 8B Applying Maslow to yourself

Reflect upon your current occupation/job. Using Maslow's hierarchy what levels do you think are normally being satisfied? What could change that would make the level move either upwards or further down the scale?

8.3.2 Herzberg's two-factor theory

Frederick Herzberg and his associates began their research into motivation during the 1950s, examining the models and assumptions of Maslow and others. The result of this work was the formulation of what Herzberg termed the *Motivation-Hygiene Theory (M-H)*. The basic hypotheses of this theory are that:

1. There are two types of motivators, one type which results in satisfaction with the job, and the other which merely prevents dissatisfaction. The two types are quite separate and distinct from one another. Herzberg called the factors which result in job satisfaction *motivators* and those that simply prevented dissatisfaction *hygienes*.
2. The factors that lead to job satisfaction (the motivators) are:
   - achievement;
   - recognition;
   - work itself;
   - responsibility;
   - advancement.
3. The factors which may prevent dissatisfaction (the hygienes) are:
   - company policy and administration;
   - working conditions;

- supervision;
- interpersonal relations;
- money;
- status;
- security.

Hygienes, if applied effectively, can at best prevent dissatisfaction: if applied poorly, they can result in negative feelings about the job.

Motivators are those things that allow for psychological growth and development on the job. They are closely related to the concept of *self-actualization*, involving a challenge, an opportunity to extend oneself to the fullest, to taste the pleasure of accomplishment, and to be recognized as having done something worthwhile.

Hygienes are simply factors that describe the *conditions* of work rather than the work itself. Herzberg's point is that if you want to motivate people, you have to be concerned with the *job itself* and not simply with the surroundings.

In a medical sense, growth, healing and development occur as natural internal processes. They are the result of proper diet, exercise, sleep etc. Hygienic procedures simply prevent disease from occurring. They do not promote growth *per se*. Herzberg says that we should focus our attention on the individuals in jobs, not on the things that we surround them with. He maintains that we tend to think that growth and development will occur if we provide good working conditions, status, security and administration, whereas in fact what stimulates growth (and motivation to grow and develop) are opportunities for achievement, recognition, responsibility, and advancement.

Once again, this theory has a basic attraction. It is always as well to bear in mind that academics, who place considerable value on autonomy and inner direction, have an obsession about making work meaningful. The notion that it is possible to realize life's true nature through creative work which is its own reward is an exceedingly attractive proposition to the learned don which is rarely fully shared by others.

Herzberg goes further than Maslow, cutting the hierarchy off near the top and maintaining that motivation results only from some elements of esteem needs and self-actualization. Having discussed Herzberg's theory try the following exercise.

EXERCISE 8C Applying Herzberg's theory

Think about your own or other people's experiences and consider the following;

1. Provide some examples where 'hygiene factors' were unsatisfactory.
2. Describe what motivators prompted a better performance.

8.3.4 **Vroom's expectancy theory**

This theory assumes that behaviour results from conscious choices among alternatives whose purpose it is to maximize pleasure and minimize pain. Victor Vroom suggested that the relationship between people's behaviour at work and their goals was not as simple as was first imagined by other scientists. Vroom realized that an employee's performance is based on individual's factors such as personality, skills, knowledge, experience, and abilities.

The theory suggests that although individuals may have different sets of goals, they can be motivated if they believe that:

- there is a positive correlation between efforts and performance;
- favourable performance will result in a desirable reward;
- the reward will satisfy an important need;
- the desire to satisfy the need is strong enough to make the effort worthwhile.

The theory is based upon the following beliefs:

Valence

Valence refers to the emotional orientations people hold with respect to outcomes (rewards). The depth of the want of an employee for extrinsic (money, promotion, time-off, benefits) or intrinsic (satisfaction) rewards. Leaders must discover what employees value.

Expectancy

Staff have different expectations and levels of confidence about what they are capable of doing. Management must discover what resources, training, or supervision employees need.

Instrumentality

The perception of staff as to whether they will actually get what they desire even if it has been promised by a leader. Leaders must ensure that promises of rewards are fulfilled and that employees are aware of that.

Vroom suggests that an employee's beliefs about Expectancy, Instrumentality, and Valence interact psychologically to create a motivational force such that the employee acts in ways that bring pleasure and avoid pain.

Vroom's expectancy theory is shown in the following figure.

Figure 8.2 **Vroom's expectancy theory**

$$\text{Valency} \times \text{Expectancy} = \text{Motivation}$$
Action
Results
Satisfaction.

Now that we can see how Vroom's theory appears to work, try the following exercise.

EXERCISE 8D

Make a list of four things that you believe motivates you at work.

Give each one a rating of 1–10 for how much you want that motivator with 10 being the one you want most. Then give each of these four things a rating from 1–10 for how likely you are to get it with 10 being very likely and 1 being very unlikely. You can write them down in the following table format.

Motivator	Valency × Expectancy = (strength (likelihood of desire) of getting it)	Motivation
1		
2		
3		
4		

Reflect upon the scores in the table above and consider whether the highest scores in the motivation column reflect what really motivates you at work.

8.4 Motivation Through Job Enrichment

Job enrichment refers to making a job more motivational and satisfying by adding variety, responsibility, and an amount of decision-making. At its best, job enrichment gives staff a sense of ownership, responsibility, and accountability and leads to a more exciting job, thereby increasing job satisfaction and motivation. In general, people work harder and are more productive when they work on tasks that they enjoy doing and find rewarding. The general idea behind job enrichment is to build into it more planning, decision-making, controlling, and responsibility. Leaders and other professionals typically have enriched occupations.

8.4.1 Qualities of an enriched job

Enriched jobs are those that contain as many of the following features as possible.

1. Direct feedback—staff should receive immediate evaluation of their work. Feedback can be built into the job or provided by the leader.
2. Client relationships—a job is automatically enriched when staff have clients or customers to serve, whether that customer is internal or external. Satisfying a customer is more satisfying than just completing a task for a manager.
3. New learning—an enriched job allows its holder to acquire new knowledge and the learning may stem from job experiences themselves or from training programmes associated with the job.
4. Control over work—the ability to have control over one's work contribution contributes to job enrichment. This can involve having some say over working hours such as flexitime, or deciding when to tackle certain problems.
5. Unique experience—this type of job has some unique qualities or features. For example, a police officer has certain powers that others do not possess, for example stop and search.
6. Control over resources—this means that the individual may have control over some or all of the resources available to carry out their job. For example, having control over money for overtime purposes, or police operations.
7. Direct communication authority—an enriched job means that staff have the opportunity to communicate directly with other people who use their output. This is similar to maintaining client relationships so, for a police officer, they can directly communicate with people who make complaints to them.
8. Personal accountability—in an enriched job, staff are responsible for their results. They can accept credit for a job well done and have to be accountable when a job is not done so well.

A highly enriched job has all eight of the features discussed above and gives the job holder an opportunity to satisfy growth needs, such as self-fulfilment. A job that appears to have some of the above would be moderately enriched, whilst a job that has none will be impoverished.

Now that we have discussed what constitutes an enriched job, try the following exercise.

EXERCISE 8E Job enrichment

Reflect upon your current job/role and try to complete the following table using the job enrichment qualities.

Job enrichment qualities	Visible in current role?	How best can I improve this?
Direct feedback		
Client relationship		
New learning		

Control over work		
Unique experience		
Control over resources		
Direct communication authority		
Personal accountability		

8.4.2 **Implementing job enrichment as motivation**

Before embarking on a programme of job enrichment the leader must ask several important questions. These would include the following:

- Do staff need more responsibility?
- Do they need variety?
- Do they need growth?

Many employees do not want an enriched job because they prefer to avoid the challenge and stress of responsibility.

8.5 **Practical Motivation**

All of the theories discussed within this chapter are valid and emphasize different approaches to motivation. As a leader you have the responsibility of ensuring that these theories can be translated into the practical policing world. You have to motivate people around you. Before moving on to further discussion, try the following exercise.

EXERCISE 8F

Think about your past and those people who have motivated you. What was it about them that did this? Write down a list of those things that made this happen.

Theories explain to us how to motivate individuals, but what happens when you need to motivate a team? Of course, teams may share a value within the group that you can use to motivate them, such as arranging a social event in order to say thank you to them for a well done job. However, these are things that perhaps good leaders do anyway when running a team. Skill in motivating others is a central leadership skill. A good leader will invariably motivate his or her team, but also individuals within that team need consideration. For example, supportive feedback or praise is usually a very effective, extrinsic motivator, but different people require different types or levels of support or feedback. Some individuals within a team will only need an occasional well-chosen word of praise which will go a long way, whilst others may need regular support and reassurance that they are doing a good job.

Leaders who listen and observe and try to understand what motivates teams and individuals will benefit. For example, when discussing future operations and plans with team members, a good leader will identify those who get enthusiastic etc. Knowing colleagues well is a good step to successfully motivating staff.

8.6 **Motivating People in Teams**

Team work has a major role to play in motivation. Identifying particular characteristics and recognizing team members as individuals in their own right as well as team members are vital to ensure that everyone works together and successfully. A good team is a group of individuals working with one another to achieve common goals, but a good leader will be aware of the characteristics of his or her team in order to be able to motivate them. It is important therefore not to view team members as all being the same type with the same characteristics. Having said that, some may have similar features and attributes to the archetypal or representative team members described in the following section.

8.6.1 **Archetypal team members**

Maitland (2001) identifies the following types commonly found within the makeup of a team. These are:

- the thinker;
- the organizer;
- the doer;
- the team worker;
- the checker;
- the evaluator.

Each of these types will now be briefly discussed.

The thinker—sometimes this person is known as the 'ideas person'. This person is concerned with the overview or what is going on and what needs to be done and provides ideas and suggestions. They may be creative but sometimes they are not very good at providing the details of how the suggestion is to be carried out.

The organizer—working with the more creative type of team member the organizer usually sorts out the practical details such as allocating tasks and duties. Sometimes a criticism of this type of individual is that they are so absorbed in doing the practical tasks etc. they can be a little dogmatic and inflexible.

The doer—this person is an individual who makes things happen. They are usually extrovert and impulsive and can sometimes dominate a team of individuals as well as being temperamental. They can become frustrated if their plans do not work out as expected.

The team worker—this person is usually eager to keep the team unified and is mostly supportive towards his or her colleagues. This person tries to develop and carry out team ideas rather than their own. In general the team worker dislikes confrontation with team colleagues and is sometimes not very noticeable.

The checker—this individual is a person who keeps a close eye on things and, as the name suggests, likes to check that everything is progressing nicely. The checker plays an important role as he or she continually reminds the team members of the need for timely completion of tasks.

The evaluator—this person is a balanced individual in between the thinker and the doer member of the team. Sometimes this individual may be slightly detached from the team and tends to analyse ideas and other suggestions carefully and objectively. The opinions of this individual are generally respected by the other members of the team.

Now that the basic types of a team have been explained try the following exercise.

EXERCISE 8G Team members

Think about your work colleagues and see if you can identify any of the above general types amongst them.

Having established the various types normally found within teams, Table 8.3 contains suggestions as to how, as a leader, you can influence them and motivate them at work.

Table 8.3 Motivating team members

Team member type	Motivation required
The thinker	Needs to be handled carefully, with praise, encouragement, and sometimes flattery otherwise they may become withdrawn.
The organiser	Needs to work in a secure and pre-planned way, so consultation about what is going to happen well in advance is required. Sometimes, provision of crime figures etc. for analysis will motivate this person.
The doer	You will need to channel the energies of this individual and prevent him or her from pressing on regardless. This requires a calming rational influence in order to channel the energies along the right lines.
The team worker	This person will need motivating by encouragement from you to partake in discussions and suggestions and to be more positive.
The checker	As a leader you will need to encourage the best parts of this type of person whilst also having to soothe his or her worries from time to time. Further, you may have to mediate between the checker and other team members as the checker's approach may cause irritation to fellow team members.
The evaluator	Because this individual tends to be slightly outside the team, the good leader will try to make him or her inclusive in the team discussions, valuing their contribution.

As with all team work, motivation requires specific skills of the leader. In brief, knowledge of the types that make up the team, along with an agreed aim and objectives, coupled with good communication between all team members will produce a well-motivated and therefore a high-performing team.

8.7 **Conclusion**

Motivation is the key to success in getting staff to perform their functions well. This applies to individuals as well as to teams such as neighbourhood policing teams, crime squads, and others. Money, social satisfaction, achievement, recognition, and intrinsically satisfying work can all be key motivators for certain people in certain situations. It is important for leaders to recognize individual differences in analysing what motivates people at work. Any theory which fails to take account of this may fail, however logical and complete it may appear.

8.8 **Summing Up**

8.8.1 **Motivators**

Motivators can be extrinsic or intrinsic. Extrinsic motivators include things from outside such as good money whilst intrinsic motivators are basic belongings for an individual such as a sense of challenge.

8.8.2 **A working definition of motivation**

There are many definitions of motivation but a useful working definition is: 'The inner force that drives individuals to accomplish personal and organizational goals.'

8.8.3 **Motivational theories**

There are several main theories that are used to help us understand what is a difficult concept and explain what motivates people in work. These are:

- Maslow's hierarchy of needs;
- Herzberg's two-factor theory;
- Vroom's expectancy theory.

8.8.4 **Job enrichment**

This idea refers to making a job more motivational and satisfying by adding variety, responsibility, and decision-making. It gives an individual ownership, responsibility, and accountability and leads to increased motivation.

8.8.5 **Team motivation**

Identifying team characteristics and recognizing that people are individuals is imperative for developing team motivation. There are several common types of individuals found in teams and, by recognizing these, the leader can play to their strengths and motivate them individually to achieve the team's aims and objectives.

References and Further Reading

Bedeian B.G. (1993) *Management Laureates: A Collection of Autobiographical Essays: v. 2 (Management Laureates)*, Pittsburgh: JAI Press Inc.

Burford, J. and Lindner, J. (2001) *Human Resources in Local Government: Techniques for Students and Practitioners*, Belmont, California: South-Western, Thompson Learning.

Herzberg, F. (1993) *Motivation to Work*, USA: Transaction Publishers.

Kovach, Kenneth A. (1987) 'What motivates employees? Workers and supervisors give different answers', Business Horizons Journal, Issue 5, 1987, 58–65.

Kreitner, R. (2007) *Organizational Behaviour*, 7th edn, Maidenhead: McGraw-Hill.

Maitland I. (2001) *Motivating People*, London: CIPD publications.

Maslow, A. (1987) *Motivation and Personality*, London: Longman Publishers.

Mullins L.J. (1996) *Management and Organizational Behaviour*, London: Pitman.

Vroom V.H. (1992) *Management and Motivation*, Harmondsworth: Penguin publishers.

Useful websites

A free website looking at motivational theory available at <http://www.business-balls.com/motivation.htm>.

A free website that considers motivation in work available at <http://www.tutor2u.net/business/people/motivation_theory_introduction.asp>.

A website that considers Maslow's work available at <http://www.maslow.com/>.

The National Police Improvement Agency website which has sections on leadership and motivation available at <http://www.npia.police.uk/>.

SPACE FOR NOTES

SPACE FOR NOTES

Dealing with Staff Issues

9.1 **Introduction**

In an earlier chapter, the transformational leadership style, which is required by all staff in today's police service, was introduced and discussed in some depth. It means that the leader will concentrate his or her efforts for the benefit of others whilst having a high degree of concern for the requirements of the organization and its service delivery. This approach can be demonstrated in a number of ways or behaviours such as 'what we do' or 'how we treat people'. Leaders need to have strong interpersonal and communication skills that demonstrate openness to change and diversity whilst also illustrating an ability to be approachable and accessible. It is important to be able to motivate, inspire, and enable staff to perform and develop. A leader needs to raise performance and reduce stress, but importantly, to show all their colleagues that they are genuinely concerned about their health and welfare.

9.2 **Staff Welfare and a Healthy Work Environment**

In the financial year that ended in March 2007, some 37,000 days were lost within the police service in England and Wales because of sickness and non-accidental injuries. The cost to the taxpayer has been estimated as being around £3 million, and is the equivalent of more than 100 officers being away from work for a whole year. The effects of this upon the remainder of the workforce is hard to calculate, but obviously if a member is away from work, then his or her share of the work has to be dealt with by others. It is against this kind of background that the Home Office published two important reports entitled 'Strategy for a Healthy Police Service' (2002) and 'In sickness and in Health: Reducing sickness absence in the police service' (2001). Both of these reports support the broad strategy that applies to all police staff and, as far as possible, to special constables. The aims of the strategy are as follows:

- the maintenance of good health in all police staff;
- the reduction of injuries and ill-health in all police staff;
- providing assistance to people who have become ill, whether caused by work or not, to return to work and full performance;
- the reduction of the number of medical retirements by managing cases of ill-health more effectively at the outset.

The strategy highlights the fact that sickness has a major impact on the efficiency of the police service in terms of absence, additional overtime costs, and stress for all staff (and their families) who are left to cover for absent colleagues.

9.3 **Responsibilities**

The documents also highlight that there are certain levels of responsibility attached to certain people. These are discussed below.

9.3.1 **Chief officers**

Chief constables and Police Authorities must ensure that, as far as possible, working conditions enable all staff to maintain good health. Chief constables must also meet their legal obligations under health and safety legislation. They must ensure that forces comply with the employment provisions of the Disability Discrimination Act 1995 for example.

9.3.2 **BCU commanders and other departmental heads**

BCU commanders and departmental heads must monitor the attendance of their staff regularly and deal effectively with poor attendance. Line managers must promote the health and safety of their staff and are responsible for managing attendance, with advice from human resources experts, occupational therapists, and health and safety specialists. This should be carried out as day-to-day working practices.

9.3.3 **Human resource managers**

Human resource managers will define the force structures, policies, and processes for managing attendance at work and will provide expert advice and support to supervisors and line managers.

9.3.4 **All police staff**

Everyone employed by the police service has a responsibility to maintain their own health. People should develop an awareness of the factors that contribute to ill-health and participate in activities to raise their own health standards.

9.4 **Targets**

Both the Home Office and HMIC are involved in the setting up and examining the results for targets in dealing with sickness levels. The Home Office will:

- publish targets for reducing sickness absence;
- co-ordinate the implementation of the strategy;
- issue guidance as it feels fit.

HMIC is responsible for:

- reviewing the performance of forces in this area;
- involving the Police Crime and Standards Directorate, which was established in 2006, where appropriate;
- working with police forces and Police Authorities to support performance improvement, and identify and disseminate good practice.

Forces are required to record and monitor sickness absence according to criteria and definitions developed by the police service. They will be expected to take the results of the monitoring into account in their human resource planning, and report figures quarterly to the Home Office. Police Authorities will use these results to inform their examination of a force's performance against strategy.

9.5 **Force Planning**

The Home Office intends that the implementation of the strategy will be built into a forces human resource plan which should be developed in consultation with the Police Authority. Each police force is expected to assess what is causing sickness absence and draws up an action plan to ensure that, as far as possible, staff do not become unwell because of work and that where they do become unwell for any reason they are helped to return to duty. In order to influence this, local policing plans should take into account national initiatives on:

- occupational health;
- ill-health retirement;
- retention of officers beyond 30 years' service.

9.6 **Causes of Absence from Work**

To manage absence effectively with targeted solutions, it is necessary to appreciate the reasons why people are taking sick leave and how long the condition may be expected to last. Recent research by Hayday et al. (2007) indicated that the causes of absence from work within the police organization were:

- In the vast majority of cases health-related with just certain individuals having attendance problems.
- For short-term absence, defined as up to 20 days, the most common causes were seen as colds, flu, and stomach upsets. Cases where individuals took short-term sickness absence for domestic and caring responsibilities were also recognized.
- Long-term absences of over 20 days were seen to be related to psychological problems (such as stress, depression, and anxiety), musculoskeletal disorders, and serious or fatal illnesses.
- Work was perceived to be a contributory factor to both short and long-term sickness when individuals felt they were under pressure due to lack of resources, bureaucratic demands, and organizational change. Sickness could also result if individuals felt that they had little or no support from the force, or were in negative work situations.

9.6.1 **Management of absence**

The majority of the responsibility for managing absence rested with the line manager and leader. For them to be effective it was necessary that the managers were:

- knowledgeable about policy and had the confidence to use their discretion to handle individuals appropriately;
- able to maintain meaningful contact with those away sick;
- well trained in absence management and in using effective inter-personal skills;
- supported by occupational health and HR.

The contributions of occupational health were vital to managing long-term absence. It was found that:

- Under-funding often led to slow or inadequate responses that could create barriers to staff returning to work.
- Line managers would like them to be more involved in short-term absence.
- Sanctions and incentives were used in all forces to encourage attendance. The sanctions were based on pay and access to training and promotion. The impact of these is unclear but staff often felt that they were unfair where individuals had ill-health or were injured. The effectiveness of incentives, such as extra leave, special payments, or recognition of good attendances by letters or certificates was perceived as variable.

Managing and maintaining a successful return to work raised some challenges:

- The timing needed to be right for the individual so they did not feel compelled to return and were not delayed by occupational health professionals resourcing issues or waiting for adjustments to be made. This is particularly difficult in cases of mental ill-health where expectations of timescales for return are unclear.
- Flexibility in how returnees work is essential and needs to be supported by line mangers and colleagues. Line managers should clarify what is expected from the returnee, set targets, and hold regular reviews.
- Recuperative duties need to be well designed and used for a limited time so that individuals get back to normal duties as soon as possible. Difficulties here were related to how the new duties were regarded by the individual and their colleagues.
- Restrictive duties were frequently misunderstood. They were confused with recuperative duties and not seen as a permanent means of retaining officers who would otherwise be retired on ill-health grounds. The increased use of these duties has led to some resentment as this reduces the number of officers that can be actively deployed.

9.6.2 **What to do during and after absence**

During an extended period of absence, a person away from work on sick leave is likely to feel isolated from colleagues and may be concerned that they will lose touch and begin to worry about returning to work. There are, therefore, ample reasons for leaders to maintain contact with that individual, besides any force policies regarding sickness that may be in being. Paying a visit to individuals at their homes in these circumstances is normally carried out by the team leader or line manager. However, it is best to prepare before carrying out a visit in these circumstances. Exercise 9A below focuses your attention on this delicate task.

EXERCISE 9A   Visiting a colleague on sick leave at home

One of the members of your team has been away from work for two weeks on sick leave. What questions would you ask yourself before making the visit? Write your answers down on a sheet of paper.

Whilst most police forces have policies on home visits for individuals on sick leave and you would obviously utilize that for guidance, you would certainly consider some of the following:

- Why is the visit being conducted?
- What is hoped will be achieved?
- Who is the most suitable person to carry out the visit?
- What stage of the illness has the person reached?
- Are they ready to discuss work issues?
- How is the person likely to feel upon arrival of the visiting person?

Sometimes, when conducting such a visit, it may become apparent that the individual needs more help and support that it is possible for you to provide. Most forces have an occupational health unit or welfare unit and it is quite reasonable under these circumstances to discuss situation with the unit and other outside agencies such as social services or the local doctor. During these discussions, you need to consider the following:

- the boundaries of your responsibilities;
- the level of confidentiality you can engage in.

9.6.3 **Returning after absence**

By effectively managing the return to work of an individual, you may be able to minimize any physical or emotional stresses for the person concerned. In this way, it may be possible to improve future attendance rates. Before moving on, try Exercise 9B below.

EXERCISE 9B   Interviewing a returnee to work

Imagine you are a person responsible for interviewing someone who is returning to work after a prolonged period of sick leave and is fit for full duties. What are some of the factors you think you will need to consider?

Having attempted the above exercise, you should have considered some of the following factors:

- Stress in the workplace, as some colleagues might make a 'joke' about people not pulling their weight and being absent.
- The allocation of a person from the team who can work closely with the individual to ease them back into full-time work.
- The need for the individual to 'catch up' on changes in the law, for example, or internal management or operational procedures.
- The individual may have identified specific development needs that you need to consider.

Throughout the re-introduction to work process, as a leader you need to consider not just short-term aims. Focus on the long-term aims, for example in three months' time you want the individual to have a full attendance record and to be engaging fully with work. However, to achieve this you will need to provide ongoing support and a periodic review of the progress of the individual concerned.

9.6.4 **Conducting the interview**

It is important that you are prepared to conduct the interview and that means being in possession of as much background information as possible. This includes any previous absences, their dates, their duration, and the reason why they occurred. The interview should be conducted in private, and Table 9.1 below illustrates a typical structure for this type of interview.

Table 9.1   Return to work interview framework

Area	Important points
Welcome	This includes an opportunity to reinforce the fact that the individual has been missed at work.
Explanation	That this is a routine activity that occurs for all people and includes the nature and structure of the interview.
Exploration	This includes asking the person about their state of health and fitness for work activity, and if appropriate to explore any underlying reasons for the absence. It may be appropriate at this stage to introduce their absence record.

Table 9.1 (*Cont.*)

Area	Important points
Planning	Here a discussion takes place concerning any further action or referral to specific departments is necessary, together with an action plan for the future.

It is important that in the course of the interview a balance be struck between the following points:

- High levels of attendance is important if targets are to be met and the organization is to function effectively.
- Showing concern and to act upon problems which the individual may have.
- Identifying future action needed such as gradual reintroduction or referral.
- Being seen to be fair and acting with sensitivity.
- Balancing the concerns of the individual with the well-being of the whole system.

There are some alternatives for the leader to consider when engaged in the reintroduction of an individual back to work. These are normally agreed at a high level, between senior management, occupational health departments, and the individual themselves. These are recuperative duties and restricted duties.

Recuperative duties—this is an opportunity to assist staff back to work full time after illness or injury, and the intention is that the person does less demanding work. For example, it may be that an officer who has been assaulted but recovering from injuries and wants to return to work may be given a temporary position in an administrative post until fully recovered for operational duties.

Restricted duties—this approach is used in some forces as an alternative to medical retirement, but can involve flexible working arrangements which are introduced where appropriate. This approach makes it possible for trained and valued staff to be retained.

9.7 **Creating a Healthy Environment**

Before moving on, try Exercise 9C.

EXERCISE 9C

Think about some of the places where you have worked or visited. What was it that you found attractive or positive, and what did you find negative about them? Write down some of your thoughts under the following headings.

Positive characteristics   *Negative characteristics*

You may have thought of something like the following:

- staff relationships;
- attitudes between staff and leaders;
- the staff turnover rate;
- the physical environment.

As a leader these factors are to some extent within your control. You as a leader will be able to have some control or influence over the nature of relationships within your team. You can regularly monitor your attitude and others and reflect upon how you may become supportive. Creating a healthy environment for work is an ideal way to use your transformational leadership skills. Changing people's attitudes can be one of the greatest challenges for a leader. Try the following exercise.

EXERCISE 9D Changing attitudes for a healthier working environment

How might you go about changing people's attitudes?

You may have considered the following approaches:

- set targets for reducing absence;
- consider more flexible working arrangements;
- involve staff in the process of improving working environments;
- make sure all staff know what is required of them;
- do not let welfare or absence problems occur without showing genuine concern and honesty.

9.8 **The Employment Act 2002**

This Act became law on 6 April 2003 and applies to all police staff. Its broad aim is to promote good working practices through fairness and partnership at work. The Employment Act has a number of measures, which will assist and guide the police leader when dealing with staff. These provisions include the following.

9.8.1 **Assisting parents at work**

The Act introduced an entitlement of 26 weeks paid maternity leave plus a further 26 weeks unpaid leave:

- two weeks paternity leave for working fathers;
- 26 weeks paid leave for adoptive parents plus a further 26 weeks unpaid leave;
- parents of children under six, or disabled children under the age of 18 years, have a right to request a flexible working arrangement.

9.8.2 **Flexibility and fairness**

- Fixed-term employees have the right to be treated as favourably as permanent staff.
- Employers will need to demonstrate flexibility to address individual circumstances.

9.8.3 **Resolving disputes**

- Altering the way unfair dismissals are judged.
- Providing efficient and swifter delivery of tribunal services.
- Encouraging more internal resolutions of disputes.
- Facilitating better understanding of the employment relationship.

Of course, as a police leader you will not know all there is to know about every aspect of employment law. However, you should be aware of the basic requirements and of the fact that there are within the police organization specialist departments which can offer support and guidance. Try the following exercise.

EXERCISE 9E Support and guidance

Consider the following circumstances and where you may turn for help and guidance within the police organization.

1. A colleague asks for advice about a career break.
2. A staff member returns to work and appears to be unfit to work.
3. A full-time worker who would like to work part-time.
4. A male colleague whose partner is expecting their first child.
5. Requests for special leave.

You have probably identified some of the following:

- the Personnel Department;
- the Human Resources Department;
- the Force Welfare Department;
- the Force Occupational Health Department.

Whichever department you contact, you will have to work very closely with them.

A workplace in which the leader practises transformational skills is one in which the staff are more likely to be supportive of the aims and objectives not only of their colleagues, but of the organization as a whole. Emphasizing the needs for high standards, this approach ensures motivation, satisfaction, and commitment.

9.9 **Controlling Stress**

Stress is used to describe something that causes us significant distress or unease. It is used in many different ways, but stress is a normal reaction and can have a positive as well as a negative effect. For example, when faced with a dangerous incident, one person will react faster to the circumstances, whilst another may not be able to react through fear. Stress factors that typically affect us can be placed into three distinct areas namely: home, work, and causes within ourselves. Now that this has been established, try the following exercise.

EXERCISE 9F

Identify some of the stress factors that may exist under each heading.

Home	Work	Within ourselves

You may have considered something like the following:

Home	Work	Within ourselves
Moving house	Change in the workplace	A desire to achieve success
Divorce or separation	Poor working relationships	Never being able to say no
Financial problems	Harassment	Low self-esteem
Bereavement	Lack of training	Taking on too much work
Changing jobs	Heavy workloads	
Illness		

Further, being a member of a minority group in the workplace may bring difficulties and pressures. Work retention rates, for example, are considerably lower within minority groups when compared to the majority ethnic staff. Try to reflect upon this and attempt Exercise 9G below.

EXERCISE 9G

List five stress factors that you think affect you, including examples from home, work, and causes within yourself.

9.9.1 Recognizing stress

Recognizing stress within oneself and, as a leader, within others is an important skill. Some of the typical behavioural and physical symptoms can be seen in Table 9.2.

Table 9.2 Physical and behavioural symptoms of stress

Physical	Behavioural
Increased use and dependency on alcohol or other stimulants	Erratic behaviour
Anxiety	Absenteeism
Raised blood pressure	Irritability
Disturbed sleep	Poor relationships with others
Digestive problems	Poor work performance

9.9.2 Dealing with stress

When considering stress it is important to consider three major points. These are:

- stress is an understandable reaction;
- stress is often a justifiable reaction;
- the causes of excessive stress should be dealt with.

Stress, therefore, is a natural and normal reaction to many situations. For the new employee joining the organization, or a student officer involved in a major police operation for the first time, there will understandably be nervousness.

Stress is often a justifiable reaction, particularly in high-risk situations. However some people find it difficult to admit that they feel nervous or even frightened, so helping staff to discuss these feelings requires some skill and sensitivity.

Supporting colleagues

Should you discover a colleague is experiencing too much or inappropriate stress, you have to decide what you can do to help. The first point is to start a discussion. The discussion is to help identify the problem, although this may not be as easy as you think. It may be that your colleague does not wish anyone to know about the problem, and of course the problem may be connected to you, the leader, and your leadership style! It may take a long time before an accurate assessment of the problem can be formulated. However, during this discussion, it is important to remember that there are a number of boundaries. To help you keep a balanced view, you should concentrate on the following:

- what you need to know;
- what the colleague wants to tell you;
- the personal skills that you have available;
- other resources and skills that are available to you within the police organization.

Despite the level of support you are offering, it will be easier for the person to confide in you if you are able to demonstrate certain qualities. Before moving on, try the following exercise.

EXERCISE 9H

Think about a time when you have supported someone in the past when they have had difficulties. Write down what qualities you believe you displayed at the time.

You may have considered that you showed some of the following qualities when you supported someone in the past:

- understanding and patience;
- being a good listener;
- being trustworthy;
- showing genuine concern;
- discretion;
- being aware of diversity and other issues.

Discussions could involve very personal issues, so there must be an understanding of confidentiality. However, the element of confidentiality can only be extended to a certain point. For example, if a colleague provides information to you in a discussion that leads you to believe that a criminal offence has taken place or that they are a danger to themselves or others, confidentiality cannot automatically be guaranteed.

These limits must be carefully explained at the beginning of any discussion, and it is always useful to keep notes of what is discussed, because you may need this record as evidence sometime in the future.

Bearing in mind the points made in Chapter 6 on meetings with staff members, consider the fact that the purpose of any such meeting is to get the colleague to talk, you may not want to make too many detailed plans in advance. However, you really need to consider some of the following points:

- what you are going to say at the beginning of the meeting;
- collecting as much information as you can, being aware that much of it may be irrelevant;
- think about the positive aspects of your colleague's work;
- possible course of actions open to you.

Consider the following information in Exercise 9I and write down your responses.

EXERCISE 9I Planning the meeting

A colleague and team member is often absent on a particular tour of duty on a particular day. You suspect that something work-related is influencing her non-attendance. Write down some responses to the points below:

1. What thoughts you may have before the meeting?
2. How can you most effectively support your colleague?
3. What action might you consider taking?

The individual would need your fullest attention, and you would need to consider what she has to say, understanding her point of view without prejudging or jumping to conclusions. The actions that you take will obviously depend upon the exact circumstances, but it is important that you be seen to take the issue seriously.

9.9.3 Managing stress

As a rule, there are three main elements to dealing with stress. These are:

- Awareness—realizing that stress is a normal reaction and recognizing what factors produce it.
- Achieving balance—finding the optimum stress level that gives stimulation and motivation but does not overload an individual.
- Gaining control—by increasing awareness and utilizing an approach of personal responsibility and assertiveness to achieve balance.

Achieving balance can be grouped under three headings, namely:

- taking action on the factors which cause excess stress;
- changing perceptions of stress;
- taking action in respect of the factors that cause stress. At least which cause colleagues to believe they are experiencing stress.

Exercise 9 J considers these points.

EXERCISE 9J Responding to stress

Think of an element of your current work or lifestyle that is increasing your stress levels. Now write down your responses below.

1. Identify what the cause of the stress is.
2. Is the stress stimulating you or are you being over-loaded?
3. If you feel overloaded:
    a. What action can you take to minimize the problem?
    b. How can you think about the situation in a different way?

Some of the responses you may have considered may have included;

- removing or minimizing the problem;
- reducing the time spent in the stressful environment;
- reorganising work to use the stress as a positive factor;
- better time management;
- seeing things from another's point of view;
- being positive in your attitude;
- changing the problem into a challenge.

9.9.4 **Lifestyle and stress**

Stress levels can be increased significantly by personal stress factors that are evident in the way we lead our lives. Write down what you think these personal stress factors may be.

Some of the factors you may have come up with could have been:

- working shifts;
- lack of exercise;
- high fat diet;
- excess alcohol;
- smoking;
- irregular eating patterns.

Having discussed these factors, try Exercise 9K below.

EXERCISE 9K Personal stress factors and yourself

Reflect upon yourself for a moment and consider what personal stress factors you may be suffering from. Draw up a list then decide upon an action plan to reduce or control the amount of harmful, personal stress you may be under.

There is now a great deal of advice on how to deal with stress, and the occupational health department or equivalent in most forces can provide this and other services. As a leader, and being in a position to identify stress in colleagues, you should now feel more confident and better able to assist other people.

9.10 **Personal Crises**

There are, unfortunately, occasions when people suffer personal crises such as a death of a family member, or a family member is taken seriously ill. This can result in the staff member reacting in a number of ways. In general, these reactions include:

- shock;
- anger;
- fear;
- helplessness;
- loss.

Whilst these reactions may be exhibited in the short term, longer-term reactions by those experiencing a personal crisis can include a loss of interest in work and home activities, a loss of personal confidence, and a loss of feeling, with an increase in irritability and anger with work colleagues and friends. These are normal reactions to an abnormal event and should be expected to occur.

9.10.1 **Handling personal crisis**

When dealing with colleagues and others who are suffering from a personal crisis, it is useful to consider the following:

- It may not be possible, or desirable, to push feelings to the back of the mind.
- Memories and feelings will not go away quickly and may even recur later.
- The way to get better is by expressing feelings, showing anger or sadness.
- It helps to share feelings with others.

9.11 **Police-Related Incidents**

A number of incidents will occur in police work that are likely to result in a high level or delayed emotional response amongst staff. These could include the death or serious injury of a police officer on duty, or a member of the public, incidents associated with suicides, murder, or child abuse, or even the loss of life after an attempt has been made to save that person. Those involved are likely to experience a number of different reactions, but it is important to remember that these are normal reactions to an abnormal situation. This is sometimes referred to as 'post-traumatic stress reaction'.

Sometimes, some individuals may experience subsequent feelings including numbness, detachment, feeling dazed, memory lapses, and the inability to relax. It is generally believed that if these types of symptoms occur within four weeks of the traumatic incident and last a few days, this is classed as 'acute stress disorder'.

Post-traumatic stress disorder (PTSD) is a type of anxiety disorder that is triggered by an extremely traumatic event. A person can develop PTSD when a traumatic event happens to them or when they see a traumatic event happen to someone else. The symptoms are similar to those of acute stress disorder but they occur over a longer period. People who suffer from this condition need to have medical help.

PTSD may affect survivors of such traumatic events as sexual or physical assault, war, torture, a natural disaster, or an airplane crash. It can also affect rescue workers at the site of mass casualties or other tragedies. These kinds of events may cause intense fear, helplessness, or horror.

9.11.1 Dealing with incidents

Once a critical incident has finished, then a process needs to occur to maintain a form of stability. This process includes the following:

1. *Defusing*. This normally occurs immediately following the incident. More than likely it is an informal process and may include only those involved and the atmosphere should be positive, supportive, and should focus on the health, care, and welfare of those involved. It should focus on an understanding that the aim is to lessen the impact and restore balance, an inquiry about what happened and how people feel and information about possible reactions to stress, additional support available, and the need for a fuller debriefing in the future.

2. *Normalizing*. This is needed when there has been a large-scale traumatic event affecting a significant number of staff. The aim is to reduce immediate stress reactions, provide information about the incident and future support, and provide a transition back to normal working.

3. *Debriefing*. Debriefing critical stress incidents is normally carried out by a trained individual and should be conducted within 72 hours of the incident. The overall aims are to:
   • help individuals to talk about their experiences;
   • help them express their emotions;
   • explain that these are normal reactions;
   • discuss future planning and coping strategies;
   • agree an action plan, which will include future support and treatment.

Of course, where necessary, referral to a specialist should be carried out as soon as possible.

9.12 **Dealing with Conflict**

Within any workplace there are bound to be occasions when conflict will emerge. This may be between the leader and the group or between members of the group themselves. When dealing with conflict as a leader, you can also draw upon the previous chapters in this book which discussed communication skills and, in particular, assertiveness and listening skills. Try the following exercise before moving on.

EXERCISE 9L

Consider the last time you were involved in a conflict situation in work or similar environment. What was the substance of the disagreement? Were you one of the people involved in the dispute or were you trying to mediate? Try to write down what you think it was all about.

By completing Exercise 9L above, you will have discovered that there is a big difference between being involved as one of the participants in a dispute and trying to act as a mediator in a dispute. Sometimes as a leader, you will experience both! One way of effectively resolving a conflict situation is by using the CUDSA process, which is effective whether you are involved in or trying to resolve conflict. The CUDSA process is illustrated below.

C Confront	the conflict by acknowledging that there is a conflict and that it needs to be resolved.
U Understand	each other's position, making clear comments about your own position and listening actively to the other person's position to clarify positions and diffuse emotions.
D Define	the problem, ensuring that all parties agree about the definition and accept that all parties will need to give ground and change position.
S Search	for and evaluate alternative solutions, mutually suggesting all the possible alternatives and make concessions and compromises.
A Agree	upon and implement the best solution.

Using the CUDSA approach shown in the above table, try the following exercise.

EXERCISE 9M Application of CUDSA

One of your team members, Jenny, has been openly criticising you because she feels that she is better qualified and would make a better leader than you. She is a long-serving member of the team, and does not think she is getting the recognition she deserves. She has recently questioned your judgement at a team meeting, and since then has realised she has over stepped the boundaries and is keeping out of the way.

What would you do, using the CUDSA model described above?

Using the CUDSA model then the first stage would be to CONFRONT the conflict. This would be completed when you decide to speak to Jenny about the situation, so you telephone her to arrange a meeting. What would you do by way of preparation for this meeting? You may consider the following:

- make sure that you genuinely want to resolve this issue and not want to vent your anger about Jenny talking about you;
- take stock of your own feelings.

Further, consider the preparation for the meeting as discussed elsewhere in this book. Consider the timing, the location, and try to ensure that you and Jenny will not be interrupted.

The meeting takes place and you sit down with Jenny. You decide to try to understand what has happened and you need to demonstrate that you have not become angry with Jenny over her behaviour, you are not a threat and that you really are prepared to sit down and talk with here about the issues. You can achieve this by being firm without appearing threatening.

In our example, Jenny tells you that she feels out of things because no-one apparently takes any notice of her opinions despite the fact that she has been here the longest. She also states that she is fed up at not being promoted despite trying for a number of years. At this point, stage two of CUDSA is being explored, as both you and Jenny are trying to understand each other's position.

There appears that there is a clear lack of understanding and communication between yourself and Jenny, and both of you agree that the problem can be positively put as 'How best can we get value out of Jenny?' You have now reached level three of the CUDSA model, that of defining the problem.

As a transformational leader, you need to consider Jenny's performance and her self-respect. Further, you may decide that you need to improve your communication skills and understand your staff better. As a result, you may decide to tell Jenny that things have not been good in the past between you and there is room for improvement in mutual understanding. Both of you decide that there needs to be ways of resolving the problem that caused the conflict—'How to get best value out of Jenny as a member of the team'. You have now reached level four of CUDSA, that of searching for evaluating alternative solutions.

When both of you agree to attempt to search for solutions, you have nearly worked your way through the CUDSA process.

Level five of CUDSA, that of agreeing upon, implementing ,and evaluating the best solutions may become the business of a future meeting with Jenny, in order to give time for ideas to formulate. When the meeting takes place with Jenny, both of you would need to consider the following points. Both of you need to:

- state agreements;
- check all is understood;
- plan, implement, and evaluate consequences;
- make a request to re-negotiate rather than just break rules;
- talk to one another.

CUDSA is a useful model for resolving conflicts and confrontation in the workplace. However, in handling such conflicts you will need to draw upon all the skills that have been discussed in various sections of this book. The most basic of these is to show concern to get the best out of people you work with.

9.13 Summing Up

9 12.1 The role of the leader in dealing with staff issues

A leader needs to raise performance and reduce stress, but importantly, to show all their colleagues that they are genuinely concerned about their health and welfare.

9.12.2 The cost of absences from police work

In the financial year that ended in March 2007, some 37,000 days were lost within the police service in England and Wales because of sickness and non-accidental injuries. The cost to the taxpayer has been estimated as being around £3 million, and is the equivalent of more than 100 officers being away from work for a whole year.

9 12.3 Stress caused by being away from work

During an extended period of absence, a person away from work on sick leave is likely to feel isolated from colleagues and may be concerned that they will lose touch and begin to worry about returning to work.

9 12.4 **The purpose of return to work interviews**

By effectively managing the return to work of an individual, you may be able to minimize any physical or emotional stresses for the person concerned. In this way, it may be possible to improve future attendance rates.

9.12.5 **Stress**

Stress is used to describe something that causes us significant distress or unease. It is used in many different ways, but stress is a normal reaction and can have a positive as well as a negative effect.

9 12.6 **Lifestyle factors and stress**

Stress levels can be increased significantly by personal stress factors that are evident in the way we lead our lives. These include our diet, drinking habits, and smoking.

9 12.7 **Post-traumatic stress disorder**

Post-traumatic stress disorder is a type of anxiety disorder that is triggered by an extremely traumatic event.

9.12.8 **The CUDSA model of handling confrontation**

One way of effectively resolving a conflict situation is by using the CUDSA process, which is effective whether you are involved in or trying to resolve a conflict. CUDSA stands for: Confront; Understand; Define; Search; Agree.

References and Further Reading

Home Office (2001) *In Sickness and in Health: Reducing Sickness Absence in the Police Service*, London: HMSO.

Home Office (2002) *Strategy for a Healthy Police Service*, London: HMSO.

Lilley, R. (2006) *Dealing with Difficult People (Creating Success)*, London: Kogan-Page.

Morrison, G. (2005) *Techniques for dealing with conflict*, Canada: Essence Publishing.

Woodward, P., Hardy, S. and Joyce, T. (2007) *Keeping It Together: A Guide for Support Staff With People Whose Behaviour Is Challenging*, Brighton: Pavilion.

Useful websites

Hayday, S., Broughton, A. and Tyers, C. (2007) *Managing sickness absence in the police service—A review of current practices,* The Institute for Employment Studies available at <http://www.hse.gov.uk/research/rrhtm/rr582.htm>.

The Employment Act 2002 available at <http://www.opsi.gov.uk/acts/acts2002/ukpga_20020022_en_1#Legislation-Preamble>.

A website that considers 10 ways to control stress available at <http://main.uab.edu/show.asp?durki=57296>.

The National Police Improvement Agency available at <http://www.npia.police.uk/>.

SPACE FOR NOTES

SPACE FOR NOTES

SPACE FOR NOTES

Leadership in Policing Teams

10.1 **Introduction**

Team working is of growing importance in many of today's organizations, none more so than in the police organization. Policing is more often than not carried out by teams of officers and other staff when carrying out their normal duties. Groups of people involved in the team approach to policing are involved in problem-solving, and this includes utilizing the community and citizens in that process. The introduction of neighbourhood policing or partnership teams across England and Wales has meant a higher profile for team leaders in the way that the service delivers to the customer. It has extended the policing family so that it is important for a leader to understand just what a team is, how it works, what types of individuals make up a team, and how best to apply the team ethic to producing an acceptable level of quality for the customer. Further, within the reform process that the police service is undergoing, there is a flattening of the organizational structure, which means that employees are gaining more authority and autonomy from top management and senior officers. This is known as empowerment where team members are entrusted to make responsible decisions at the front end of policing without referral to senior officers on every occasion. First, though, we need to understand just what constitutes a team.

10.2 **What is a Team?**

Some senior officers use the term 'my team' when they refer to all those people who have to report to them. However, does this make all those people one team? Before moving on, write down what you think a team is.

You may have thought of teams in terms of sport. What makes them a team rather than a group of individual players? When we consider a group of people, we can differentiate them from a team as groups are always forming and reforming in organizations for a number of different reasons such as:

- to get work done as a project group or committee;
- to meet for social needs such as interest groups, hobby groups, or sports pastimes;
- to meet interest needs such as staff unions.

Therefore, a group can be defined as a group of people or objects considered as a collective unit. They may be brought together formally, for example as a committee, or informally between individuals with similar interests.

Definition of a group

A group of people or objects considered as a collective unit.

Teams are groups of people who share a common objective and agree how to pursue that objective. The characteristics of a team are as follows:

- teams have a specific task or goal in common;
- team members are committed to the task;
- a team develops its own identity based upon its members' combined personalities;
- team members must work together to achieve their goal;
- team activity needs to be co-ordinated;
- team members regularly become involved with each other.

Having seen what characteristics make up a team, try to complete the following exercise.

EXERCISE 10A

What work teams can you identify?

Teams and their style vary widely as their formation, tasks, the style of operation, and their leadership creates different sorts of teams which carry out different functions.

On the one hand, there may be the formal team, which will have a defined purpose and a framework within which it operates and members may have structured roles. This is often seen as a work department formed by a mixture of people joining and leaving the department over time to carry out related work.

Because of the recruiting process of the police, many team leaders and members come from different and varied backgrounds. This, coupled with the fact that some people work full-time, others part-time, some are police officers with full powers and no official union representation, whilst others are unsworn officers, such as community support officers, and support staff with full union representation and different work-related contracts, makes the creation of teams a challenging yet rewarding task.

The diversity of team members, however, should be regarded in a positive light. Team members will bring different levels of knowledge and work experiences and different skills and approaches to problem-solving and will reflect the diverse make-up of society.

Definition of a team

Teams are groups of people who share a common objective and agree how to pursue that objective.

10.2.1 **Leadership and teams**

Leading teams is different from leading individuals and this is because of the different internal activities and interactions that take place between individuals within the team. The internal processes can normally be divided into distinct areas. These are:

- task;
- management;
- transactional;
- mechanisms, systems, tools and resources;
- people;
- leadership;
- transformational; and
- motivation.

Team leaders are responsible for ensuring that the processes are helping and not hindering the achievement of the group. One model that illustrates the balancing act that a team leader has to achieve is functional leadership. In this approach, the leadership function can be illustrated as three overlapping areas of work. This can be seen in Figure 10.1 below.

Figure 10.1 Functions of a leader

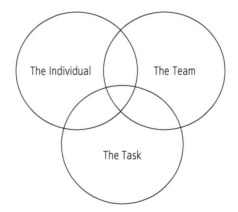

This approach shows that the effective leader has to:

- achieve the task;
- develop the individual;
- build and maintain the team.

With this information in mind, try the following exercise.

> **EXERCISE 10B Types of leaders**
>
> Consider the different types of leader and what would happen if a leader tended to concentrate only on one particular area. For example:
>
> 1. The leader focuses almost completely on tasks.
> 2. The leader focuses almost completely on individuals within the team.

You may have thought of some of the consequences of concentrating too much on one particular area as being:

- individual team members would feel devalued if the leader concentrated solely on tasks; and
- not much would be achieved if the leader concentrated only on the development of individuals within the team.

10.2.2 Team development

Teams do not normally start out as an efficient, well-oiled instrument to deal with agreed aims and objectives. In the main, there is a process of evolvement, which can sometimes be painful, that a team has to go through before they are fully developed. Tuckman (1972) produced a model of team development that describes the stages that a well-formed team needs to go through. This can be seen in Figure 10.2 below.

Figure 10.2 A model of team development

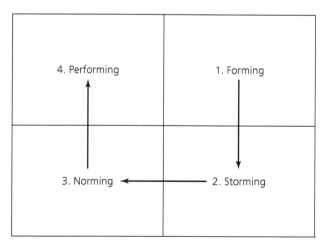

Each of these stages is discussed below.

1. *Forming*. This normally occurs when an individual or individuals join a team that already exists or when a group comes together. Often it is here that mis-understandings occur as the initial adjustment period takes place, and leaders try to stamp their authority whilst team members try to assess them.
2. *Storming*. At this point, feelings tend to come out into the open, and the focus of the team is upon inner conflicts between members. The team tends to react poorly when it comes under pressure, and often certain team members act as peacemakers to try to resolve issues within the team.
3. *Norming*. This stage sees the introduction of ground rules that are accepted by every team member, and working procedures are internalized and agreed upon. Closer working relations between group members are established based upon trust and mutual respect.
4. *Performing*. Now the team displays a high level of flexibility and commit-ment to team goals using a problem-solving approach. Conflict is dealt with constructively and in a positive manner with issues being resolved through consensus.

Some people may say that there is a fifth element to this process and that is *mourning*. This occurs when a team is disbanded. For the leader this is an impor-tant area also. The leader should ensure that when the team disbands or when a team member leaves, that this is seen in a positive light, and aimed at bringing a sense of appropriate closure to the incident. Failure to deal with this stage of team development can result in the team becoming unsettled and other mem-bers wanting to leave through declining morale.

10.2.3 **Team behaviour**

The success of teams depends upon how people behave and interact with the processes that occur within the team function or approach. A good team leader needs to ensure that the team's aims and objectives are achieved whilst also ensuring that individual team members and their morale are supported. Figure 10.3 below illustrates some of the key interrelated factors that a leader must lead in order to ensure team effectiveness.

All of the factors illustrated in Figure 10.3 rely upon good open communica-tion within the team. For example, a leader who wishes to ensure that group standards such as dress code are established and agreed upon has to communi-cate them to others. Similarly, a member who becomes unusually quiet may be de-motivated or un-cooperative because of personal problems or problems with others within the team. Such problems need to be confronted and resolved, and the leader's duty to treat all staff fairly and without discrimination and ensure that others maintain this standard is of paramount importance.

Figure 10.3 Factors that affect team performance

Source: Adapted from Berry et al 1998.

10.2.4 **Team cohesiveness**

Cohesiveness means the attraction of members to the group or team. The most important effect of cohesiveness for work teams is that their members cooperate more and their productivity tends to increase, especially where the work involves interacting with customers. Working teams can last a long time. During this time, the social system of the team develops slowly. One of the most important aspects of this system is the cohesiveness of the team—the extent to which the group members are attracted towards the group and its aims and objectives. With the passage of time, a team is more likely to become more cohesive, though some teams become more so than others, and the process can take place quite quickly. Cohesiveness can be measured by feelings of loyalty or pride, such as in the detection of crimes, and the relative frequency of the words 'we' and 'I' or the amount of helping that takes place within the team. Now we know what cohesiveness is, attempt the following exercise.

EXERCISE 10C Increasing effectiveness of teams

Imagine you are in charge of a work team. What would you do to try to increase the cohesiveness of your team?

There are several causes of cohesiveness. These include:

- Physical proximity. This tends to result in more friendships and in people seeing themselves as groups.
- The same or similar work. Where team members are engaged in similar work, for example the work carried out by neighbourhood policing teams, and then because they are faced with the same or similar problems, they tend to help each other in many ways.
- The workflow. Cohesiveness is increased if the workflow, or type of work, brings together members of the team in a rewarding or cooperative manner. Cohesiveness is greater in teams when they are able to communicate easily with each regarding their work.
- The group bonus scheme. When a team has a shared group goal, such as the reduction in the number of burglaries, or the prevention of anti-social activity within their area, then the efforts of the team will be concentrated towards those goals. This means that individual team members will promote the interests of other team members.
- Leadership styles. Democratic styles of leadership and encouraging group participation in decisions increases cohesiveness.
- Size of teams. If a team is too large it will divide into two or more sub-groups, usually based on differences of status, work etc. Absenteeism, for example, appears higher in large teams.
- Team development. Developing skills of team members through the problem-solving approach and setting goals appears to increase the cohesiveness of teams.

10.3 Delegation to Team Members

Delegation is a key function for a police leader. Of course, a leader will often allocate tasks to others, sharing out workloads to fit into an individual's competence, experience, and availability. However, this is not delegation. Delegation involves giving authority to a team member to carry out a task, which the leader would normally do. The team member then becomes responsible for the task, whilst the leader remains ultimately accountable for the success or failure of the task. A leader can delegate authority but not responsibility.

KEY POINT—DELEGATION

Delegation involves giving authority to a team member to carry out a task, which the leader would normally do. The team member then becomes responsible for the task, whilst the leader remains ultimately accountable for the success or failure of the task.

Delegation is a skill that some people find difficult to master. This is sometimes because people are used to dealing with issues themselves and then they know if it is being done properly. Sometimes a leader will think that the other team members are too busy and if work is delegated then they will become overloaded with work. However, despite some of these ideas, the effective leader will have to delegate to ensure that they can fulfil the requirements of their role. Successful leadership is getting work done through others. Exercise 10D asks you to consider the advantages and disadvantages of delegation in teams.

EXERCISE 10D Advantages and disadvantages of delegation

Write below at least three points for each heading.

Advantages of delegation   *Disadvantages of delegation*

Having completed the above exercise, compare your thoughts to the following.

10.3.1 **The advantages of delegation**

As a result of successful delegation:

- the leader is able to concentrate on high priority tasks;
- the moral of the team member rises if they are given suitable extra responsibilities;
- team members are trained to carry out new duties;
- team members and leaders increase their job satisfaction.

10.3.2 **The disadvantages of delegation**

In the main, the disadvantages of delegation appear to affect the leader. These include:

- enjoyable parts of the job may have to be given to others to do;
- initial preparation for delegation with staff members can be time consuming;
- leaders can lose some feeling about what is going on because of having to stand back;
- team leaders may feel a little threatened, especially if the team member completes the task apparently better than the leader.

Delegation should be considered as a learning experience for both the leader and for the team member. The most important point about delegation is clarity. Clear communication with the team member is essential so that they fully understand the objectives, scope boundaries, and the expectations for the job that has been delegated.

10.4 **High Performing Teams**

Some teams perform much better than others do. One way of remembering why good teams do this is to use the mnemonic PERFORM. This stands for:

P	**Purpose**	A good team has a common purpose, with plans and good clear goals and roles allocated to team members.
E	**Empowerment**	Team members feel they are adequately prepared for their role and are fully supported by the team leader and other members.
R	**Relationships**	Team members freely communicate with each other and value, accept, and listen to the other person's views and opinions.
F	**Flexibility**	Each team member can perform a different role as needed and can adapt and explore new ideas.
O	**Optimal Productivity**	The teamwork rate is high, with excellent quality, as the team members are allowed to make decisions and solve problems as necessary.
R	**Recognition**	Individual and team contributions are valued, appreciated, and respected by all.
M	**Morale**	People feel good about themselves, the team and the job they are doing. Consequently, they feel motivated and have a strong team spirit.

Having discussed the nature of teams, their formation, and how to delegate as well as other facets of leading teams in the police, the following part of this chapter highlights one of the most important visible team approaches in modern policing, the introduction of neighbourhood policing teams. It illustrates just how the aims and objectives of teams are linked to the wider backcloth and theories that underpin policing such as the extended policing family, citizen-focused policing, problem-oriented approaches, and the signal crime approach.

10.5 **Neighbourhood Policing and Teams**

One of the most high profile police team initiatives is the introduction of neighbourhood policing teams. The concept of neighbourhood team policing appears quite straightforward. It is about dealing with crime and disorder more intelligently and building new relationships between the police and the public. This relationship should be one built on co-operation rather than mere consent. It relies upon local people being part of the solution to local problems of crime and disorder. First, however, we need to understand what a neighbourhood means.

The answer is that for the purposes of neighbourhood policing teams it depends upon many factors. These include:

- crime statistics,
- housing information,
- employment information.

In addition, there are many other social factors not just a political ward or group of houses.

To a person living in the inner city, the idea of neighbourhood may seem different to someone living in a country village. A whole council may appear to be a neighbourhood in one instance, whilst in some areas it can mean a political ward.

The government, in pursuing this initiative, has suggested that the definition of neighbourhood should be left up to local communities, police forces, and authorities and their partners rather than being told by themselves. Therefore, what comprises a neighbourhood for policing teams will differ in different parts of the country.

Now that we realize that a neighbourhood is not quite as simple as we thought, we need to consider who will make up the neighbourhood policing team.

Well, the police of course, but who else do you think might be part of this new team approach to local community and problem-solving? In Exercise 10E below, consider who you think may make be part of the team.

EXERCISE 10E The make up of teams

Police officers		Community representatives	
Police community support officers		Volunteers	
Police specials		Neighbourhood watch	
Private security guards		Parish or neighbourhood wardens	
Community intelligence		Traffic wardens/road officers	

The answer is that all of the above will be a part of the new neighbourhood policing teams, which will target specific problems identified by close liaison with communities throughout the country.

The way the team may operate can be seen in Figure 10.4 below.

Figure 10.4 A typical neighbourhood team

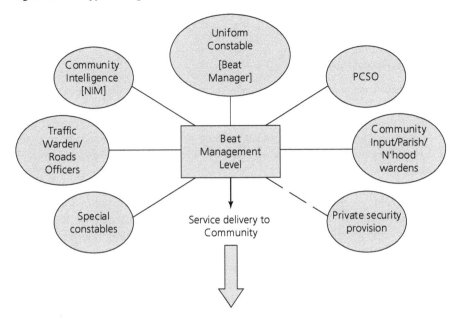

The idea of neighbourhood policing teams tackling crime and anti-social behaviour has been seen in several parts of the country already. This approach should be much more than just high visibility reassurance policing. It uses local knowledge and intelligence from local people to target crime hotspots and disorder issues causing most concern to local communities. The government has stated that the latest technology will support the initiative including the issue of mobile telephone numbers to individuals within neighbourhoods so that they can contact the local beat manager directly.

Neighbourhood policing teams mean that people will:

- *know who their local police officers are* and how to contact them;
- have a *real say in local policing* issues and setting local priorities; and
- *know how well their police are doing* locally in tackling crime and anti-social behaviour.

Neighbourhood teams are an excellent example of delivering police services through a variety of different people, not just sworn police officers. The group of people engaged in this activity are often referred to as the extended policing family.

10.6 **The Extended Policing Family**

We have seen from the Police Reform Act 2002 (Home Office 2002) that substantial change is in store for the police service and it is this Act that enables us, with some accuracy, to predict the future delivery of policing. The introduction of police community support officers, coupled with the use of neighbourhood watch and local warden schemes, will introduce a more flexible method in dealing with community problems, even if at this stage they may lack sufficient powers to carry out their full role. The extended police family, responsible for ensuring the tackling of day-to-day policing of crime and disorder, is worthy of exploration.

10.6.1 **Uniformed constable**

The role of the uniformed constable is crucial in that he/she will act as the 'manager' of the co-ordinated service delivery. This enables the constable to perform a more proactive role in consultation, co-ordinating delivery through the various officers available, and where necessary being available to use the full powers available to a police constable. The role dramatically alters the idea of constable from one of enforcer of laws only to that of facilitator and leader. This will require a more professional approach and therefore perhaps a more highly qualified individual to perform the role. The constable, it is envisaged, will be directly accountable to his/her line supervisor, the sergeant, who will have responsibility for two or more of the policing teams.

10.6.2 **Police specials**

The powers owned by police specials, who are volunteers, are the same as for regular officers. They receive the same amount and level of training as regular officers, wear the same uniforms, and provide invaluable support in many situations. As volunteers, they are able to offer only a certain amount of their time. Despite this fact, they should, if their availability is intelligently managed, provide useful high visibility patrol, backed up with the lawful authority to use force if necessary, just like regular sworn police officers.

10.6.3 **Police community support officer**

The police community support officer (PCSO), working with the other members of the delivery team, will be used not only to provide reassurance through visible patrolling at relevant times, but also through use of his/her powers to resolve low level community problems. They will provide the beat manager with invaluable assistance in dealing with minor instances of public disorder and anti-social problems.

10.6.4 **Traffic wardens**

With the idea of traffic wardens not only enforcing road traffic offences but also being able to issue fixed penalty notices for certain other offences, this role becomes a vital part of the integrated policing system. They can further operate as a means of obtaining information for the policing team, supplying criminal and community intelligence through their visible presence on the street. They will be available to deal with local traffic problems as well as being involved in maintaining safety on the roads.

10.6.5 **Parish or neighbourhood warden schemes**

Whilst originally conceived as an eyes and ears approach for the police, coupled with concierge and reassurance functions, these warden schemes may well be able to issue fixed penalties for various offences such as minor criminal damage (graffiti) to the depositing of litter. The increase in surveillance and reassurance by high visibility patrolling that these schemes provide will be an invaluable asset to the beat manager.

10.6.6 **Private security provision**

It is possible that within the neighbourhood teams idea use could be made of private security officers to enhance the policing capability. Whilst the main function of private security industry has in the past been the protection of private property, there has been an increase in their use for such roles as prisoner escort, as well as other custody duties assisting sworn officers. The Private Security Industry Act 2001, which regulates the industry, will have wide repercussions for the use of private security in the public domain of policing. The main areas of current activity include the roles of wheel clamping, guarding premises, and as security consultants. Section 40 of the Police Reform Act 2002 introduces the community safety accreditation scheme that is designed to extend limited police powers to persons already engaged in community safety duties. These include local authority wardens as well as security guards within private security industry.

10.6.7 **Volunteers**

A clear theme of the current government agenda for reform and modernization of the public services is the development of new ways of involving local communities in shaping the priorities and outputs of public service delivery. This involves identifying new and less formalized methods of communication between the public services and service users to make delivery of services more responsive to the needs of local people. Generally speaking, the police service in England and Wales has a modest record in the involvement of volunteers in its activities. The special constabulary has been the principal initiative and significant effort has been put into recruitment, retention, and empirical evaluation of the business and community benefits of using these volunteers.

10.7 Citizen-Focused Policing

Citizen-focused policing has been highlighted as a key priority in the National Policing Plan 2005–08 and is considered fundamental to the future and direction of police reform. It is therefore important to understand what exactly it means for the police service and policing anti-social behaviour.

10.7.1. Why involve citizens?

Involving citizens in the way policing services are delivered will, it is hoped, provide forces with a greater understanding of their communities, thereby increasing the public's confidence and satisfaction with the police. By adopting this approach, the police service will become reflective, considering the impact of the way police services are delivered from the perspective of the citizen. It follows, therefore, that the public should have a greater say in how policing is delivered and become more involved in the delivery of services by the police. Policing will become a joint effort between citizens and police, removing the traditional notion of policing by consent, but introducing policing by active cooperation. The aim is to replace a passive public as consumers of police services over which they have little or no say, to a situation where local communities can actively support their police service and have a say in how and contribute to the way they are policed.

10.7.2 Are there any problems with involving citizens?

This approach may have more problems than some believe. Police services, as we have seen, can traditionally have a very strong organizational culture that builds walls around itself in an effort to protect itself from 'outsiders' (see Reiner 2000 and Holdaway 1984 for examples of this). There sometimes appears to be a belief that the police 'know best'. However, this will not necessarily meet the public's need, and police officers have to recognize this, and when making decisions they have to consider the citizen's perspective.

The public must be acknowledged as being more than just users of a service. They are stakeholders who should be continuously engaged with by the police in order to provide an effective and efficient police approach to community concerns, especially crime and disorder.

10.8 **The Problem-Solving Approach**

Problem-Oriented Policing (POP) is a recent innovation that is closely associated with the concept of community policing and is inspired by the work of Herman Goldstein (1990). POP tries to replace the call for police service with the 'problem' as the basic unit of police attention. Thus, POP focuses on the crime and disorder 'event' and analyses why it should have occurred. This is a major change in the way policing has traditionally been delivered.

Tilley (1997:1) attempts to explain the philosophy behind Goldstein's work by using the following story taken from Goldstein (1990):

> Complaints from passengers wishing to use the Bagnall to Green Fields bus service that drivers were speeding past bus queues of up to 30 people with a smile and a wave of the hand, have been met by a statement pointing out that it is impossible for the drivers to keep to their timetable if they have to stop for passengers.
>
> (Tilley 1997:1)

This is a simple example of a problem with modern-day policing. Pre-occupation with the smooth running of the organization for its own ends can come to take priority over the fulfilment of the purpose for which the organization is there in the first place. Goldstein's (1990) work on problem-oriented policing is concerned with ensuring the police keep their 'eye on the ball' and that the ball encompasses the concerns that the public brings to them. These concerns in general tend to be problems that affect their quality of life. Therefore for the police, *all business* the public brings to the *police is police* business not just crime. POP is about taking seriously all the problems the police are there to deal with. This involves:

- looking out for problems systematically from police data, other agency data, and contact with the communities served;
- trying to analyse the problems to find their underlying causes;
- attempting imaginatively to intervene to address underlying causes that are realistically open to change;
- setting up systems to learn about what works, how, for whom, and in what circumstances in dealing with problems;
- feeding lessons back into growing problem-oriented wisdom within the police service.

10.8.1 **POP and traditional policing**

POP, like community-oriented policing, is another step away from the traditional reactive, and stand alone, approach to policing. The following illustrates the main differences.

- POP enables the police to be more effective. At the moment, the police spend a lot of time responding to calls for service. Rather than just attending call after call, POP offers the police a way for addressing the underlying conditions that create the calls in the first place.

- POP allows police officers to utilize the experience gained over a number of years to resolve problems in a creative and effective manner.
- POP entails the involvement of the wider community to make sure that the correct problems and concerns are addressed. These are the bedrock of long-term solutions to identified problems.
- Much of the information required to provide long-term solutions to problems are not just held in police records. Partnerships with other agencies play a major part in the problem-oriented approach to policing.

Again, this approach can pose problems for the police culture, as it opposes the strict law enforcement model that tends to predominate police thinking. Resistance from individuals can thwart good intentions. As Goldstein says: 'Over and over again I have seen first line supervisors whose relationship with their subordinates reinforces the notion that the police function consists of going in and getting out as fast as you can' (Mulraney 2000b: 22).

What is also needed is a new form of supervision that makes it legitimate to take the time to get beyond simply applying emergency treatment to a problem and moving on to the next problem with the same approach.

POP and communities

POP is an important development for the police, especially when engaged in partnership work. In the past, the police were considered the experts in policing and needed very little, if any, assistance. They were regarded as the professionals and should be left alone to get on with their job. The reality is the police cannot get the job done by themselves. They need all of the resources of various agencies that contribute to crime reduction and control of anti-social behaviour. The police need the help of the community and other agencies if problem-solving initiatives are to be successful.

Under the POP approach, police officers are encouraged to explore new avenues, to introduce creative alternatives in their use of a wide range of methods for preventing or reducing problems. This includes altering the physical environment, mediating disputes involving the community, employing civil law, and bringing other local authority services or regulatory agencies to bear.

10.8.2 Analysing problems

In order to identify repeat problems and to try to solve them using the appropriate resources, scanning technology, and the ability to use it must be of the highest order. This, until recently, was not readily available to most police forces in this country. The assumption was that whilst perhaps forces wanted to be involved in problem-solving, the ability to deliver it effectively was not seen in practice. This was emphasized by Read and Tilley (2000) who highlighted the weakness in the ability to analyse information and data-sharing limitations as being major obstructions to successful problem-solving. However, most police forces now operate with specially trained staff that analyse information at Basic Command Unit level and perform this valuable role in identifying crime hotspots and community problems. The 'problem' is therefore an important part to this policing approach. The Key Point box below considers just what a problem is.

KEY POINT—CONSTITUENT ELEMENTS OF POP

A problem is considered to be the basic unit of police work—rather than one crime, case, call, or incident. A problem is a group of crimes, cases, calls, or incidents.

A problem is something that concerns or causes harm to citizens—not just the police. Things that concern only police officers are important, but they are not problems in this sense of the term.

Addressing problems means more than just quick fixes; it means dealing with the conditions that create problems.

Police officers must routinely and systematically investigate problems before trying to solve them—just as they routinely and systematically investigate crimes before making an arrest.

The investigation of problems must be thorough, even though it may not need to be complicated. This principle is as true for problem investigations as it is for criminal investigations.

Problems must be described precisely and accurately, and broken down into specific aspects of the problem. Problems often are not what they first appear to be. Problems must be understood in terms of the various interests at stake. Individuals and groups of people are affected in different ways by a problem.

Having identified what the problem is, then steps have to be taken to solve it. One important way of achieving this is through the use of the Problem Analysis Triangle.

10.8.3 Analysing the problem

Sometimes it can be difficult to see how a particular problem can be solved. The Problem Analysis Triangle (sometimes referred to as the crime triangle or PAT) provides a way of thinking about recurring problems of crime and disorder. The PAT was derived from the routine activity approach to explaining how and why crime occurs (discussed elsewhere). This theory argues that when a crime occurs, three things happen at the same time and in the same space:

- A suitable target is available.
- There is the lack of a suitable guardian to prevent the crime from happening.
- A motivated offender is present.

Therefore, we see that this idea assumes that crime or disorder results when (1) likely offenders and (2) suitable targets come together in (3) time and space (location). The PAT is illustrated in Figure 10.5 below.

Figure 10.5 A simple Problem Analysis Triangle

Location

Offender

Problem

Victim or Target

10.8.4 Responding to the problem

However, whilst this triangle concentrates on the analysis of the problem, we can add another outer level for each of the three original elements. This helps us consider how to *respond* to the problem we have identified by considering a controller for each of them.

If we consider the victim or target element of the PAT above, we can add the control element of *guardian*, usually people who protect their property etc.

For the offender element , this control is called the *handler*, someone who perhaps knows the offender well and who can exert control over them. This could include parents, friends, teachers, husbands, wives etc.

Finally, in terms of the original element of location the controller is called the *place manager*. This is someone who has responsibility for the place and could include janitors, teachers , bus conductors etc.

Consequently, our simple PAT now looks like that illustrated in Figure 10.6 below.

Having examined the PAT and the definition of problems, consider the circumstances in the exercise below and apply the triangle to this incident.

EXERCISE 10F Applying the Problem Analysis Triangle

A number of complaints have been received from residents in a neighbourhood regarding the congregation of youths at an old-fashioned stone-built bus shelter every evening between 7pm and 11pm. Passengers at the bus stop feel intimidated whilst residents nearby complain of noise and litter left at the bus stop. Further, there is a nearby infants school, and it is alleged that minor damage is being caused as a result of the youths congregating.

Figure 10.6 A simple Problem Analysis Triangle

As you can see, once the PAT is applied and the three elements explored many options appear that can be explored to provide an answer to the 'problem' highlighted in the exercise.

By using the PAT and applying the broad principles of POP to this information, we can consider the following responses:

- What do the youths have as an alternative to the shelter? (The Location)
- Has anyone actually spoken or consulted with them? (The Offender)
- What facilities can the infants school offer regarding an alternative to the bus shelter as a shelter for the youths? (The Location)
- What can the bus company/local authority do regarding the use of the bus shelter? (The Location)
- What consultation has taken place with the community, especially near the bus shelter? (The Victims)
- Is there anyone in the community who can offer youth mentoring or youth club facilities? (The Victim)
- Why are the youths congregating at this location at this time? (The Offenders)

Of course you should also consider what other agencies can be involved in this process. The point to note is that the triangle allows you to examine problems in a more structured manner.

10.9 The SARA Model of Analysis

A commonly used problem-solving method is the SARA model (Scanning, Analysis, Response, and Assessment). It can be used to identify underlying causes of problems and how they may fit into a wider pattern of similar problems. It can also help the police practitioner and prevent him or her jumping straight to a response that may be the wrong one. The SARA model contains the following elements.

10.9.1 Scanning

Problems are identified through a wide range of data and other information including local police knowledge, intelligence, crime reports, and public information and help to build up information for later analysis. Here, problems become grouped or clustered.

KEY POINT—THE SCANNING PROCESS

- Identifying recurring problems of concern to the public and the police.
- Identifying the consequences of the problem for the community and the police.
- Prioritizing those problems.
- Developing broad goals.
- Confirming that the problems exist.
- Determining how frequently the problem occurs and how long it has been taking place.
- Selecting problems for closer examination.

10.9.2 Analysis

Here the details of the problem are examined in more detail. Scanning might tell us that a large amount of criminal damage is taking place, but analysis will tell us the times, dates, methods, types or property damaged, witnesses, suspects etc. It is at this stage that information from partner agencies should be incorporated, which will provide alternative perspectives and extend the possibilities of finding trends and patterns.

Analysis therefore is seen in the following Key Point box.

KEY POINT—ANALYSIS

- Identifying and understanding the events and conditions that precede and accompany the problem.
- Identifying relevant data to be collected.
- Researching what is known about the problem type.
- Taking stock of how the problem is currently addressed and the strengths and limitations of the current response.
- Narrowing the scope of the problem as specifically as possible.
- Identifying a variety of resources that may be of assistance in developing a deeper understanding of the problem.
- Developing a working hypothesis about why the problem is occurring.

10.9.3 **Response**

This stage involves the implementation of suitable action to resolve the problem. It can involve the assistance of other agencies and partnership members where appropriate. Responses to problems may be multi-layered, involving police action against a suspect, victim support for individuals or groups of people, and changes to the geographic location where offences have occurred, eg the introduction of street lighting, CCTV cameras etc. The response stage is summarized in the Key Point box below.

KEY POINT—RESPONSE TO PROBLEMS

- Board blasting for new interventions.
- Searching for what other communities with similar problems have done.
- Choosing among the alternative interventions.
- Outlining a response plan and identifying responsible parties.
- Stating the specific objectives for the response plan.
- Carrying out the planned activities.

10.9.4 **Assessment**

This is the evaluation phase where the effectiveness of the response to the problem is evaluated. Here, the decision is made as to whether the objectives have been met. Assessment should consider not only the effects of the response but how it was used. For example, there may have been more than sufficient resources available for the task, yet the result was not as positive as would have been expected. The assessment stage involves the following:

KEY POINT—ASSESSMENT

- Determining whether the plan was implemented (a process evaluation).
- Collecting pre- and post-response qualitative and quantitative data.
- Determining whether broad goals and specific objectives were attained.
- Identifying any new strategies needed to augment the original plan.
- Conducting ongoing assessments to ensure continued effectiveness.

Figure 10.7 below illustrates the SARA process.

For any response to crime and disorder to be effective, it must rely on a strong and systematic process of analysis of the underlying problems and their causes. The PAT and the use of SARA are two of the most commonly and successfully used items in problem identification and problem solving.

There is growing evidence that crime and disorder incidents can cluster in ways that are identifiable by these methods. They are sometimes referred to as signal crimes and this area is intrinsically linked to policing crime and disorder as

Figure 10.7 The SARA process

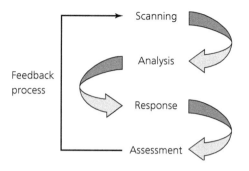

they call for particular police and other agency intervention. Signal crimes have a direct influence on community perceptions about crime and disorder and are worthy of the attention of the police practitioner.

10.10 **Policing Signal Crimes**

The signal crimes perspective is an important idea that can inform reassurance style or high visibility policing. In summary, it states that:

- Some crimes and disorders act as warning signals to people about their exposure to risk.
- These signals impact on the public's sense of security.
- They cause people to change their beliefs and/or behaviours to adjust to the perceived risk.
- The perspective covers a whole spectrum of crimes and disorders.
- The perspective gives an opportunity to target those problems that matter most to the public.
- Police and their partners can establish 'control signals' to neutralize signal crimes and signal disorders.

The main idea behind signal crimes is to focus upon how people react to crime and disorder and how they attribute meaning to their experiences of these types of social problems. In essence, it is an approach that understands crime and disorder as having communicative properties, with people interpreting the various incidents that they encounter to construct judgements about the levels of risk that are present. What appears to happen is that some crime and disorder matters more than others in terms of communicating a sense of risk to the public. This is because certain incidents have a higher '*signal value*' than others. For most people much crime and disorder functions as little more than background 'noise' to the conduct of their routines in everyday life. However, certain incidents have far more significance to them—these are signal crimes and signal disorders.

10.10.1 **Visibility and context**

There are two factors that explain why some incidents function as signals, namely visibility and context. Context refers to the ways that the contextual conditions in which crime and disorder occur shapes whether an incident will function as a signal to the public or not. Communities are more or less resilient to different types of social problems, depending upon their socio-economic and demographic make-up. Thus, the social context in which a problem occurs is a significant influence in terms of whether people will view it as a signal or not. Relatedly, the visibility of an incident will help to determine whether it functions as a signal—if people are unaware of the presence of a crime or disorder it cannot function as a signal to them. In some instances, the visibility of a problem is amplified by media coverage. However, enhanced social visibility may also occur through people encountering a problem directly on a regular basis. This latter dimension helps to explain why people routinely attribute high degrees of significance to problems of incivility and anti-social behaviour occurring in their neighbourhoods. It is believed that by targeting activity to those incidents of crime and disorder that have a particularly high 'signal value' the police can achieve a disproportionate impact in terms of tackling the problems that are especially generative of a sense of public insecurity.

10.10.2 **Reassurance policing**

The concept of control signals also provides an important link between the signal crimes perspective and reassurance policing. The emphasis upon control signals identifies a need for police to ensure that their activities are visible to the people they serve, if they are to reassure them about levels of safety. Thus, one justification for the police engaging in highly visible foot patrol activities is that it can function as a potent control signal to members of the public. Uniformed foot patrol signifies to people the presence of an authoritative figure that can be called upon to restore social order should it be disrupted in some way. An aim of reassurance policing is to find ways of identifying and acting against risks in the local neighbourhood that have a disproportionate impact upon people's experiences and perceptions of security. Thus, the signal crimes perspective provides a mechanism for thinking about how this objective can be achieved. Through a combination of targeting signal crimes and disorders, and ensuring the presence of visible control signals, the police in partnership with other local agencies and communities can act to improve levels of neighbourhood security.

10.11 **Conclusion**

Teamwork is an essential part of policing. Leadership of policing teams requires individual skills and knowledge of how a team forms, how it performs to a high standard, how it need to be cohesive, and how the leader has to delegate and develop team members. The neighbourhood policing team initiative and its underpinning ideas about community engagement, problem solving, signal crimes, and public reassurance highlights the importance placed upon teamwork in tackling crime and disorder within communities.

10.12 **Summing Up**

10.12.1 **Definition of a group**

A group of people or things considered as a collective unit.

10.12.2 **Definition of a team**

Teams are groups of people who share a common objective and agree how to pursue that objective.

10.12.3 **Effective leadership**

The effective leader has to:

- achieve the task;
- develop the individual;
- build and maintain the team.

10.12.4 **Development stages of teams**

- Forming.
- Storming.
- Norming.
- Performing.

10.12.5 **Team cohesiveness**

Cohesiveness means the attraction of members to the group or team. The most important effect of cohesiveness for work teams is that their members co-operate more and their productivity tends to increase, especially where the work involves interacting with customers.

10.12.6 **Delegating to team members**

Delegation involves giving authority to a team member to carry out a task, which the leader would normally do. The team member then becomes responsible for the task, whilst the leader remains ultimately accountable for the success or failure of the task. A leader can delegate authority but not responsibility.

10.12.7 Good teams PERFORM

This stands for:

P Purpose

E Empowerment

R Relationships

F Flexibility

O Optimal Productivity

R Recognition

M Morale

10.12.8 Neighbourhood policing teams

One of the most high-profile police team initiatives is the introduction of neighbourhood policing teams. The concept of neighbourhood team policing appears quite straightforward. It is about dealing with crime and disorder more intelligently and building new relationships between the police and the public.

10.12.9 Citizen-focused policing

Involving citizens in the way policing services are delivered will, it is hoped, provide forces with a greater understanding of their communities, thereby increasing the public's confidence and satisfaction with the police.

10.12.10 Signal crimes

The signal crimes perspective is an important idea that can inform reassurance style policing. In summary, it states that:

- Some crimes and disorders act as warning signals to people about their exposure to risk.
- These signals impact on the public's sense of security.
- They cause people to change their beliefs and/or behaviours to adjust to the perceived risk.

- The perspective covers a whole spectrum of crimes and disorders.
- The perspective gives an opportunity to target those problems that matter most to the public.
- Police and their partners can establish 'control signals' to neutralize signal crimes and signal disorders.

10.12.11 **Problem-Oriented Policing**

Problem-Oriented Policing (POP) is a recent innovation that is closely associated with the concept of community policing and is inspired by the work of Herman Goldstein (1990). POP tries to replace the call for police service with the 'problem' as the basic unit of police attention. Thus, POP focuses on the crime and disorder 'event' and analyses why it may have occurred.

10.12.12 **SARA**

A commonly used problem-solving method is the SARA model (Scanning, Analysis, Response, and Assessment). It can be used to identify underlying causes of problems and how they may fit into a wider pattern of similar problems.

References and Further Reading

Argyle, M. (1990) *The Social Psychology of Work*, London: Penguin Books.

Berry G, Izat, J., Mawby, R., Walley, L. and Wright, A. (1998) *Practical Police Management*, London: Police Review Publishing Company.

Blanchard, K. (1993) *The One Minute Manager Builds High Performing Teams*, London: Harper-Collins.

Goldstein, H. (1990) *Problem Oriented Policing*, New York: McGraw-Hill.

Holdaway, S. (1984) *Inside the British Police:* A Force at Work, London: Blackwell.

Home Office (2001) *The Private Security Industry Act*, London: HMSO.

Home Office (2002) *The Police Reform Act*, London: HMSO.

Mulraney, S. (2000) 'Making Your Mind Up', *Police Review* 16/9/00 p 22.

Reiner, R. (2000) *The Politics of the Police* (3rd edn), London: Harvester Wheatsheaf.

Tilley, N. (1997) *'Problem Oriented Policing'*, IEA Seminar Papers, London: IEA.

Tuckman, B.W. (1972) *Conducting Educational Research*, New York: Harcourt Brace Jovanovich.

Useful websites

The National Policing Improvement Agency available at <http://www.npia.police.uk/>.

Articles on leadership available at <http://www.theleadingarticles.com/cid62/Leadership/>.

Teamwork website available at <http://reviewing.co.uk/toolkit/teams-and-teamwork.htm>.

The national website for Neighbourhood Policing Teams available at <http://www.neighbourhoodpolicing.co.uk/>.

The Problem Oriented Policing website available at <http://www.popcenter.org/>.

SPACE FOR NOTES

SPACE FOR NOTES

SPACE FOR NOTES

Leading Operations

11.1 **Introduction**

A leader in the police organization will attend many situations which will demand important decision-making. Whilst those decisions are being made, the leader will have to consider not only their own safety, but also the safety of all staff and of course the public. Early decisions may well influence or affect the final outcome and may make the difference between life and death.

Given the variety of situations that the police have to deal with, it is impossible to provide a framework for dealing with everything that happens. This is because every situation is different and it would impinge on the discretion of the leaders when it comes to decision-making. It is the leader's ability to manage every different incident effectively which is crucial for a successful outcome.

This chapter will introduce you to the idea of police operations and how the police organization plans and responds to them. First, we need to consider what we mean by a police operation. Think about this for a few moments and see if you can answer the question in Exercise 11A.

EXERCISE 11A

What is meant by the term 'Police Operation'? Write down your thoughts.

You may have thought of a few events such as a major sporting occasion or a royal visit. In many senses you would be right. An operation within the police service, however, can mean almost anything. It can range from unforeseen disasters involving loss of life such as a plane crash or terrorist bombing, to dealing with local issues such as a parade or a large village fete.

11.2 **The Role of Gold, Silver, and Bronze**

Obviously, when operations are carried out, either pre-planned or response to emergency type operations, there needs to be a structure in place to ensure that all that needs to be done is carried out. In general terms the command structure for an operation has three distinct levels of command. These commands are called:

- Gold;
- Silver; and
- Bronze.

Each of these levels of command has a different function to perform in the supervision of an operation. Table 11.1 below illustrates the role of each level of command.

Table 11.1 Levels of command

Command	Main role and function
Gold Command	This person is very often of quite high rank, eg Chief Superintendent, and is in charge of the whole operation. Gold decides what the goals are for the operation, eg to arrest a particular individual or to ensure that a protest march is allowed to take place with little disruption. This person delegates carrying out the goals to Silver Commander.
Silver Command	Silver commander has responsibility for determining just how the goals identified by Gold Commander are to be carried out. This is known as forming the tactics for the successful completion of the operation. Silver commander is sometimes the responsibility of a Superintendent or Chief Inspector.
Bronze Command	Bronze commander operates at the 'ground level' of the operation ensuring that the tactics devised by Silver command are carried out. Very often this commander is of Inspector rank although it is sometimes carried out by a sergeant.

Whatever rank the commander or other participants are, the underlying idea behind the planned operation is that of teamwork. Whatever your role within the operation or organization, each person is as important as the other when it comes to reaching a successful conclusion.

11.3 **Specialist Units in the Police**

The police service contains many different specialist units. The use of these units is of great importance to the police when they plan an operation. The aims and objectives of an operation determine the type and number of different specialist units and members of the wider policing family that will be deployed. For example, a drugs raid on a house means that at least part of the operational team will include drug squad officers and maybe a drug sniffer dog, as well as other officers used to carry out various roles such as securing the scene and the recovery of evidence and material. Further consideration may need to be taken of inclusion of non-police specialist personnel such as social services if children are in the house.

In the following exercise, consider the different types of police roles required for the operations described. The first example is completed for you.

EXERCISE 11B Police roles and operations

Type of pre-planned operation	Resources to be deployed
A drugs raid on a house where illegal drugs are being sold and the occupant is known to be uncooperative.	1. Specialist forced entry team. 2. Community support officers for securing outer cordon around the general area. 3. Specialist arrest teams dependent upon the number of people expected to be in the house. 4. Drug squad members trained in the search and recovery of drugs and other material/evidence. 5. Specialist dog and dog handler trained in detecting hidden drugs.
A political demonstration outside a military base.	
The planned arrest of a suspect as a result of a long enquiry into numerous sexual offences against children.	

11.4 Why do the Police Mount Pre-Planned Operations?

There are a number of reasons why the police mount operations. The carrying out of operations generally involves quite a number of police personnel who are utilized away from their normal duties, so there has to be good reasons for their re-deployment. The following exercise asks you to think of some of the sources of information that would lead to the use of planned operations.

EXERCISE 11C

Make a list of the sources of information that might lead to pre-planned police operations.

Some of the more common sources of information include the following:

- calls or information from the public;
- advanced warning from organizers of events;
- the decision to make arrests following an investigation;

- decisions made by the tasking and coordinating groups that are part of the National Intelligence Model process.

The use of the National Intelligence Model is considered to be of prime importance in the use of pre-planned police operations.

11.5 **The National Intelligence Model**

The National Intelligence Model (NIM) is a model that ensures information is fully researched and analysed to provide intelligence that the police can use to inform strategic thinking, make tactical decisions about resourcing and operational policing, and helps to manage the delivery of policing. One important point to note is that the model is not just about intelligence, it can be used for most areas of policing. For example, it sets the requirements for the contribution of patrolling, reactive, proactive, and intelligence staff. Community and criminal intelligence will be of importance if the police are to respond to crime and disorder, as well as policing other events, effectively. Consultation with the community at this level, through formal structures such as regular meetings with representatives from the community and surgeries for the public to attend and air their concerns, coupled with sophisticated community intelligence available to the police will be effective tools in the drive to sustain order maintenance.

KEY POINT—THE NATIONAL INTELLIGENCE MODEL

'The Model has real value in that it clearly outlines the component parts of the intelligence process and clarifies terminology which is all too often misunderstood. Adoption of the model throughout the UK will ensure commonality in working practices and an understanding of the intelligence requirements which will ensure greater effectiveness in the future.'
(John Orr, OBE, QPM (NCIS 2000))

NIM is a major introduction in the context of police reform. NIM is a model that ensures information is fully researched and analysed to provide intelligence that senior police managers can use to inform strategic direction, make tactical decisions about resourcing and operational policing, and helps to manage risk. One important point to note is that the model is not just about intelligence, it can be used for most areas of policing. It is first and foremost, however, a business process model. It is dependent upon a clear framework of analysis of information and intelligence allowing a problem solving approach to law enforcement and crime prevention techniques. The expected outcomes are improved community safety, reduced crime, and the control of criminality and disorder, leading to greater public reassurance and confidence. The following figure illustrates the NIM process.

Figure 11.1 A simplified schematic model of the National Intelligence Model

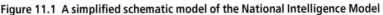
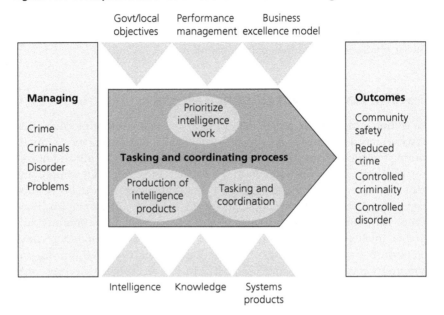

NIM is the product of work carried out by the National Criminal Intelligence Service on behalf of the Crime Committee of the Association of Chief Police Officers (ACPO). The model has been designed to have an impact at three levels of police activity, namely levels 1, 2, and 3. These levels are explained in the following box.

KEY POINT—LEVELS OF ACTIVITY IN NIM

Level 1—Local issues which are the crimes, criminals, and other problems affecting a basic command unit (BCU). This area will encompass wide issues such as low level theft to murder, and it is anticipated that the handling of volume crime will be at this level.

Level 2—Cross-border issues that affect more than one BCU. This may include problems that affect a group of BCUs or neighbouring forces, and may also involve support from the National Crime Squad, HM Customs & Excise, or the NCIS. Common problems, the exchange of data and provision of resources for the benefit of all concerned will be key issues at this level.

Level 3—Serious and organized crime which usually operates on a national and international scale will be dealt with at this level.

In terms of local partnerships, the Tactical Tasking and Co-ordinating Group (Tactical T & CG) comprises a chairperson and a small group of senior managers who have responsibility for one BCU and who can make resourcing decisions. Part of their function is also to consider corporate intelligence products which may impact upon their area as well as being represented at force level.

11.5.1 The role of intelligence in setting pre-planned objectives

One of the most vital ingredients in a pre-planned operation is the setting of clear objectives. In order to ensure that the objectives are the right ones, intelligence gathered from the NIM process and other information helps to formulate them. For planned events, gathering information is easier because there is more time. If intelligence is to be gathered using covert methods, it is important to remember that this is covered by the Regulation of Investigatory Powers Act 2000 (RIPA).

Defining objectives

Consider the following information and try Exercise 11D. You receive information from the force control room that a female customer in a local fast food takeaway restaurant has been assaulted with what appears to be a glass or bottle. Prior to the assault, the female was threatened by another female who has left the scene.

EXERCISE 11D Immediate actions and objectives

Knowing the information above, write what your first thoughts and actions would be.

Some of the things you may have considered could have been:

- safety of victim, public, and the police;
- medical attention for victim;
- collection of information from scene;
- resources available to deal with incident;
- scene management;
- crime scene management (in particular, the first 'Golden Hour' of any investigation where so much evidence can be gathered).

The process above starts the leader on the path to setting objectives for the control and dealing with the incident. However, the objectives should be as simple as possible, and any more than three would be difficult to manage. It makes sense to prioritize your objectives, but this is not as simple as it seems. However, when we consider the initial objectives for the scenario illustrated above, we can categorize them as follows:

- risk assessment of scene;
- preservation of scene;
- need to inform others.

Another way of looking at this problem is to ask yourself an important question, namely, what is the main reason for being here? Obviously the answer is safety, and gathering evidence. In summary, Figure 11.2 shows the main areas you should be considering when setting objectives for dealing with incidents.

Figure 11.2 Points to remember that will help set objectives

1. State in simple terms what you want to achieve (objectives).
2. Your objectives are balanced.
3. Your objectives are lawful and lie in the area of core police business.
4. The risks involved have been examined.

11.6 Using SCENE and CHALET for Unplanned Events

One way of responding to serious and unplanned events is by using the mnemonics SCENE and CHALET. This way you can respond through a framework that will enable you to cover the most important aspects of what they *initially* need to do at the scene of a major incident. For example, using the information given below, write down how you would respond to receiving the information.

EXERCISE 11E Write down what you think you should do

You are on duty at midnight on a Friday night when you receive a report of an assault in the local high street. A male person has been seriously assaulted by what appears to be a baseball bat. The offender has left the scene.

At first perhaps you may think of such things as getting an ambulance, going to the scene, and finding out what happened. These are all natural reactions and none of them are wrong. However, to help ensure that the correct response is applied to the incident, the police turn to a mnemonic called CHALET. It is quite an easy mnemonic to remember. The definition of CHALET can be seen in Figure 11.3 below.

Figure 11.3 CHALET

C Casualties	Approximate no. of casualties: dead, injured, not injured
H Hazards	Present and potential: debris, terrain, chemicals, fire, danger
A Access	Best routes for emergency services, suitable RV point
L Location	Ensure precise location of incident known to all concerned
E Emergency Services	What other resources do you require—how you can get them
T Type	Accurately establish type of incident, its extent, number of people, vehicles, buildings etc.

Using the information in Figure 11.4 below, try to apply this to our example of the assault in the High Street in the following exercise. The first two boxes have been completed for you.

EXERCISE 11F Applying CHALET to an incident

Casualties	One male person, apparently seriously injured by a baseball bat.
Hazards	In the street, people possibly intoxicated and perhaps not, availability of other weapons i.e. glasses and bottles, witnesses and culprit left scene.
Access	
Location	
Emergency Services	
Type	

As you can see, this framework will help you consider how to respond to an incident and also what you need to do and who to contact. It also provides a well thought-out response that covers the important issues at the beginning of an unplanned serious incident.

Having done so, the police need to consider the wider response to unplanned incidents as they may have to use other emergency services such as the Fire and Rescue department or the Ambulance service. Again, there is a useful mnemonic to assist in this process. This is called SCENE. This is an easy mnemonic to remember as it relates to the scene of the incident itself. The definition of SCENE is shown in Figure 11.4 below.

Figure 11.4 SCENE

S Seal area	Seal off area, establish cordons, provide access routes, control persons entering, rescue is a priority.
C Control	Establish a control point, and possible a joint emergency control point, issue identification tabards, ensure a log is maintained.
E Emergency Services	Co-ordinate their arrival, provide escorts if needed.
N Notify	Control room of actions, be accurate, clear and concise. Be prepared to brief others and to be briefed by specialists.
E Evacuate	The injured. If serious risk, evacuate the scene, leave the dead.

If we consider our original information about the disturbance and serious assault in the high street, we could apply SCENE to this set of circumstances. This is illustrated below in Figure 11.5.

Figure 11.5 Application of SCENE

Seal area	The high street has now become a crime scene. Therefore the scene will need to be preserved. Cordons may have to be put in place and officers placed at certain points to restrict access.
Control	Contact the operations room so that the control room supervisor is aware. Establish one person at the scene to receive radio calls and mobile phone calls in the initial phases. One police officer or police community support officer may be designated to record decisions in a log of events.
Emergency services	Ensure the ambulance knows where to attend. If injury is life threatening enquire with ambulance service as to whether they need escort.
Notify	Keep control updated with information. There may be the need to inform specialist squads or teams to take over the enquiry. Briefing of other personnel is an important job that you may have to consider.
Evacuate	Ensure all injured are evacuated from the scene. In our scenario, you may have considered a police officer to attend the hospital with the casualty to obtain as much information as possible.

The mnemonic SCENE and CHALET are quite useful in responding to any type of *unplanned* incident in the early stages. How the police deal with known and planned events is discussed below.

11.7 **Pre-Planned Operational Information**

The way that police staff are briefed for operational activity is very important. The briefing and how it is communicated can dictate how successful the operation may turn out to be. Some people find it very difficult to brief one or two individuals let alone large numbers of people. A common problem with briefings is that they may be too long or contain too much information. People are on the whole only able to absorb about seven items of information at one time so we need to remember this when preparing our briefing. Practice is obviously important, but remember, *proper practice prevents poor performance! (The 5 Ps)*. For pre-planned operations a good format that can be used is one which uses the mnemonic IIRMACC. This mnemonic provides for a very useful framework when it comes to planning an organized event. IIRMACC stands for the following;

I Information	What we know about the event, venue, who is coming, what the allegations are etc. Any intelligence brief will be updated on a separate sheet.
I Intention	How we intend to police the information, for example, in line with the chief constable's policy or guidelines to minimize disruption to the public etc.
R Risk Assessment	For example the threat level of security of event or incident. The likelihood of public disorder. It may be the likelihood of injury through dangerous animals, insecure buildings, weapons etc. We have seen earlier how we can identify and manage risks for the safety of everyone involved in the operation.
M Method	This section relates to how the event will be policed. Who will do what and when and how? Policies regarding the 'what if factor', eg a pitch invasion at a major sporting event may need to be considered here. Perhaps cordons will need to be established. The deployment of specialists would come under this heading.
A Administration	Here we need to consider such items as tours of duty for individuals concerned. Also what is the mode of dress? Perhaps full uniform for royal visits for example, or full riot clothing for major disturbances. Overtime claims forms and their submission. Exhibits and their recording by designated officer.
C Communication	Important information such as what radio channels are to be used is indicated in this section. Further, we need to consider where the control room is located and who will operate it. Consideration about such matters as where radios are to be booked out and returned to,

	the issue of mobile phones and their numbers should also be placed in this section.
C Community Impact Assessment	This is a very important section and may be completed as a separate document and attached to the briefing document. It considers how the operation will affect the community. For example prolonged closing of roads, the impact of stop and search on ethnic minorities within the target area, and the impact upon a community's fear of crime may be some issues for consideration. Consultation with local community leaders should be considered here as well as the impact on partnership members, eg drug rehabilitation workers after drugs raid.

Let us look at a scenario in the light of the IIRMACC framework. Using the information provided in the following exercise, consider some of the following:

EXERCISE 11G

The police are told that a man is dealing drugs from his home address, which is situated opposite a school. Intelligence suggests that he has a rotweiler dog which he keeps in order to protect his drugs, which are stored in a box beneath the floorboards in the front room of his home. Write down how you think you would carry out this pre-planned operation. What do you believe are the important things you need to consider and how would you plan for them?

Figure 11.6 below illustrates some of the areas that could be considered using the IIRMAAC approach.

Figure 11.6 The IIRMAAC approach

Information	Intelligence on the suspect and associates. Information about the numbers of people on the premises. Layout of the building. Previous information about the premises. Entrance and exit routes.
Intention	To gain safe entry, to contain the suspect and others people in it. To gather evidence on entry, and to locate and arrest drugs offenders.
Risk assessment	Make aware of risks/hazards such as drugged people, violent offenders, and the rotweiler dog and potential weapons, eg glasses, whereabouts of school pupils and staff.
Method	The instructions given to staff including how entry is to be made, the deployment of staff to particular jobs, gathering of evidence, dealing with any prisoners, equipment required and its location, covering of exits etc.

Administration	Briefing times, dress to be worn by staff, eg full riot gear by entry teams may be a possibility, the numbers of staff required, dedicated control team, amount of force to be used, injuries on duty, welfare, and refreshments.
Communication	It may that different radio channels may be used for the duration of the operation, and certain mobile phone numbers need to be disseminated. It could also include different code names assigned to different individuals/teams.
Community impact	Preparation of a media release, meeting with community leaders to calm the community, liaison with school staff.

All police pre-planned orders must comply with human rights legislation and must be proportional in its response to the problem, and respect individual's rights under the Human Rights Act 1998. (Home Office 1998)

Having seen how this approach can be used to formulate a briefing for a pre-planned operation, try to apply this information to the following exercise.

EXERCISE 11H

Information has been received that a small demonstration is to take place outside a meat packaging factory by a group who think it is inhuman to eat meat. They are not expected to cause any disturbances but they will number around 30 people. The factory is situated on a busy B-class road which has lorries travelling along it quite frequently.

11.8 Principle Objectives in Firearms Incidents

Whenever the police receive a call regarding a firearms incident, the objectives should remain that of the safety of the public and police, at the scene and elsewhere and gathering evidence. However, the principle objectives in any firearms situation should be that illustrated in Figure 11.7 below.

Figure 11.7 Principle objectives in firearms situations

Identify . . .	Who the suspect is by name and description.
Locate . . .	Where the suspect is.
Contain . . .	The suspect and surround the location. However, SAFETY is paramount.
Neutralise . . .	The threat from the armed suspect by the SAFEST possible means.

It is important to remember that your role as a leader is not to operate by yourself but to enable your colleagues to operate. A large part of the leader's role is to keep others informed. You may:

INFORM   BCU staff, tactics advisor, control room, surrounding BCUs, other emergency services.

NOMINATE   staff for BCU cover, supervision for BCU cover.

PREPARE   briefings for others due to arrive at the scene, plans of the area, space for specialist units, eg Armed Response Vehicles.

11.9 Handing Over

There will be some situations where you as a leader will deal with an incident or operation from start to finish. However, this does not happen all the time and the handing over of an operation or incident to another person may take time. It is important that the handover is completed efficiently or the effectiveness of the operation may be compromised, and good work carried out at the beginning may be lost. The type of incident that this may involve could be one of the following:

- a firearms incident to a tactical firearms officer;
- a major incident to a senior officer;
- a serious crime to an SIO (Senior Investigating Officer);
- a long-term operation such as a pop festival planned for a weekend or a search for a missing person.

The successful setting of objectives and the gathering of information at the beginning of the incident now proves to be very useful at this point. If you know you are going to hand over at a particular point in time, then you can consider the type of questions that you are going to be asked. Exercise 11I considers this point.

EXERCISE 11I

Imagine you have been the leader at an operational incident whereby there has been a very serious assault during the night shift. You know that the Detective Chief Inspector will be on duty at 6 am. Write down a list of the factors you consider to be important to achieve a successful handover.

Hopefully, you would have considered some of the following factors:

- be concise and to the point;
- be clear in what you say;
- have clear objectives;
- make a risk assessment;

- if personnel may need to be changed during the incident, make sure that this clear;
- ensure administration is correct and clear;
- have all the information written down;
- summarize what ahs been done and achieved;
- Highlight what is outstanding in terms of things to be done.

11.10 **Debriefing Operations**

At the conclusion of any operation, whether pre-planned or not, it is always useful to conduct a debrief of the event. The reasons why a debrief is carried out are as follows:

- It summarizes information following an incident.
- It identifies good working practices.
- It ensures all information is disseminated to all those involved.
- It also identifies poor working practices.
- It identifies points for learning/development for future operations.
- It motivates staff and can be used to praise them.
- It identifies any support required for staff as well as any training needs.

It is important that all staff involved in the operation are brought together for the de-brief session. There are several important areas that a debrief needs to cover. These include such things as who attended the incident, where did it happen, what happened, why it happened, what was learned, and how will it affect future actions.

This can be shown as a typical debrief model below.

Figure 11.8 Model for debriefing staff

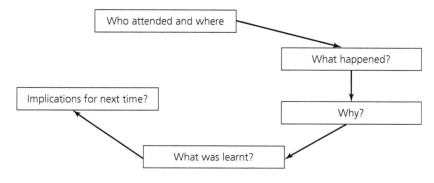

This approach is very similar to that known as the experiential learning cycle, with the purpose of identifying good practice and also ineffective practice. The idea is to see whether we can learn for the future. This does not just have to be any negative aspects of the incident, but also the positive aspects that can be highlighted as good practice. This is a simple model to remember and can be adapted in its use for any type of de-brief.

11.11 Conclusion

In this chapter, you have been introduced to the different types of operations that police staff have to manage and lead. They are useful tools for any type of pre-planned operation or for confronting emergency and unexpected incidents. However, as a leader, what must be remembered at all times is the safety of the public and staff when engaging in these types of activities.

11.12 Summing Up

11.12.1 Operations

An operation within the police service can mean anything from unforeseen disasters to dealing with local issues.

11.12.2 Command structure

Command structures in either pre-planned or response type emergencies are called Gold, Silver, and Bronze.

11.12.3 The National Intelligence Model

The National Intelligence Model (NIM) is a business process model that seeks to ensure that information is fully processed and analysed to provide intelligence that is used to inform strategic and tactical decisions. It operates at three levels, namely local, force, and national.

11.12.4 SCENE

SCENE is a mnemonic that helps provide a framework for the response to unplanned events. It is commonly used in conjunction with another mnemonic CHALET.

11.12.5 IIRMACC

This is a mnemonic that is used by the police as a framework for briefing staff for pre-planned operations.

11.12.6 **Principal objectives in firearms incidents**

The principal objectives in firearms incidents are: Identify, Locate, Contain, and Neutralize.

11.12.7 **Debriefing**

At the conclusion of an operation a debriefing session should be carried out to review the operation and inform future activities.

References and Further Reading

Rogers, C. (2006) *Crime Reduction Partnerships,* Oxford: Oxford University Press.
Newburn T., Williamson T. and Wright, A. (2007) *Handbook of Criminal Investigation*, Cullompton: Willan.

Useful websites

A useful website looking at technology supporting police operations available at <http://scienceandresearch.homeoffice.gov.uk/hosdb/police-equipment-technology/supporting-police-operations/>.

HMIC website concerning all aspects of Police Health and Safety available at <http://inspectorates.homeoffice.gov.uk/hmic/ptd/guidance/pol-hs.pdf>.

Government website dedicated to responding to all types of emergencies available at <http://www.ukresilience.info/>.

The specialist operation centre at National Police Improvement Agency available at <http://www.npia.police.uk/en/5219.htm>.

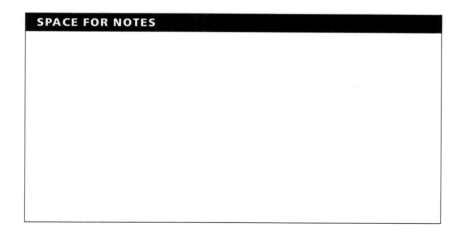

SPACE FOR NOTES

SPACE FOR NOTES

SPACE FOR NOTES

SPACE FOR NOTES

Index